UP AGAINST WHITENESS

UP AGAINST WHITENESS

Race, School,
and
Immigrant Youth

Stacey J. Lee

FOREWORD BY
Lois Weis

Teachers College
Columbia University
New York and London

Published by Teachers College Press, 1234 Amsterdam Avenue, New York, NY 10027

An earlier version of Chapter 2 was published as S. J. Lee, "Learning 'America': Hmong American High School Students." *Education and Urban Society, 34*(2), 233–246. Copyright © 2002 by Sage Publications. Reprinted by permission. All rights reserved.

An earlier version of Chapter 3 was published as S. J. Lee, "More Than 'Model Minorities' or 'Delinquents': A Look at Hmong American High School Students." *Harvard Educational Review, 71*(3), (Fall 2001), 505–528. Copyright © 2001 by the President and Fellows of Harvard College. Reprinted by permission. All rights reserved.

Library of Congress Cataloging-in-Publication Data

Lee, Stacey J., 1962–
    Up against whiteness : race, school, and immigrant youth / Stacey J. Lee; foreword by Lois Weis.
        p. cm.
    Includes bibliographical references and index.
        ISBN 0-8077-4575-8 (cloth : alk. paper) — ISBN 0-8077-4574-X (pbk. : alk. paper)
        1. Hmong American teenagers—Wisconsin—Social conditions. 2. Asian American high school students—Wisconsin—Social conditions. 3. Immigrants—Wisconsin—Social conditions. 4. Hmong Americans—Ethnic identity. 5. High schools—Social aspects—Wisconsin. 6. Racism—Wisconsin. 7. Racism—United States—Case studies. 8. Wisconsin—Ethnic relations. 9. Wisconsin—Race relations. 10. United States—Ethnic relations—Case studies. 11. United States—Race relations—Case studies. I. Title.

    F590.H55L44 2005
    305.235'089'95942073—dc22

                                                                                2004065909

ISBN 0-8077-4574-X (paper)
ISBN 0-8077-4575-8 (cloth)

Printed on acid-free paper

Manufactured in the United States of America

12 11 10 09 08 07 06   8 7 6 5 4 3 2

FOR MY GRANDPARENTS

Contents

Foreword by *Lois Weis*   ix

Acknowledgments   xiii

1 Becoming Racialized Americans   1

   Race and Asian American Immigrants   3

   Assimilation Theories Reconsidered   7

   The Hmong in the United States   11

   In the Field   16

   Road Map for the Book   21

**2 At University Heights High School:
Creating Insiders and "Others"**   23

   Inside the Halls of UHS   25

   *A Matter of "Culture":
Interpretations of Hmong American Students' Experiences*   41

3 "Traditional" and "Americanized" Hmong Students   50

   "Two Groups of Hmong Students"   51

   Constructing Identities Against Each Other   53

   "Traditional" Hmong Youth: The 1.5 Generation   55

   "Americanized" Hmong Youth: The Second Generation   65

   Conclusion   86

4 Wimps, Gangsters, Victims, and Teen Moms:
   The Gendered Experiences of Hmong American Youth   **87**

   Dominant Messages About Gender   88
   Ideal Masculinities and Femininities at UHS   89
   Wimps, Gangsters, Victims, and Teen Moms:
     Perceptions of Hmong Youth   90
   Messages About Gender from the Hmong
     American Community   95
   Constructing Hmong Femininities in the United States   98
   Constructing Hmong Masculinities in the United States   113
   Conclusion   121

5 Race and the "Good" School   **123**

   Revisiting Theories of Segmented Assimilation   124
   Making "Good" Schools   126

References   **131**

Index   **143**

About the Author   **153**

Foreword

Since the 1970s, forms of ethnographic investigation in schools have become increasingly popular. We now have excellent studies of the on-site production of culture and identity in both schools and community centers. Such studies range from those targeted at the White working class (Everhart, 1983; Foley, 1990; Weis, 1990; Willis, 1977), students of African descent (Dimitriadis, 2003; Fine, 1991; Ogbu, 1974; Solomon, 1992), White women of different social classes and backgrounds (Luttrell, 1997; Proweller, 1998), students of Asian descent (Centrie, 2004; Lee, 1996), to those of Latino background (Valenzuela, 1999). Such work has expanded our knowledge on how youth from varying social classes and ethnic/racial backgrounds go to school and "become somebody" (Wexler, 1987), developing identities inside specific institutions and locations.

Michelle Fine and I (2004) recently explicated what we call "compositional studies," a theory of method in which analyses of public and private institutions, groups, and lives are lodged in relation to key social and economic structures. We call for deep ethnographic work within a particular group; serious relational analyses among relevant bordering groups; and penetrating analyses of broad structural connections to social, economic, and political arrangements, thereby suggesting that the remaking of any given society and a group's or individual's position within such society can only be understood through a clear focus on the bordering "others," as well as historically based social and economic trends (Weis, 2004).

Herein, Stacey Lee offers a brilliant "composition," reflecting the three tenets of theoretical and analytic considerations outlined above. Lee does the deep ethnographic work exceptionally well. She offers a well-drawn portrait of the Hmong in a Midwestern school, bringing this relatively unknown group to life for her readers as they go to school and traverse the boundaries dividing family and community. But Lee does so much more than this, and here is where her ethnographic composition stands above so many others. Drawing on her carefully conducted ethnographic investigation, she uses her scholarly sense and keen analytical eye to understand how global and national formations and relational interactions seep through the lives, identities, and communities of youth and adults,

ultimately refracting back on the larger social formations that give rise to
them. Lee's accomplishments are impressive, especially since it is relatively
easy to write institutional stories as dense, local qualitative descriptions,
without revealing the webs of power that connect institutional and individual lives to larger social and economic formations.

It is the Hmong set *inside* the broader context of the global economy,
the segmented racial structure of the United States, and the ways in which
such structures interconnect with the production of "Asian" youth in general and Hmong youth in particular that distinguishes this volume from traditional ethnographies. Lee's careful attention to gender, social class, and
the production of racial factors—specifically whiteness, blackness, and varying forms of becoming Asian-American—render this work a cut above all
others. Lee makes it clear that the production of varying Hmong cultures
and identities within schools cannot be understood outside the social and
economic context in which such production occurs. That the Americanized
Hmong who dress in hip-hop clothing are considered "blackened" by both
the school and the Hmong community can only be understood in the context of a racist America where being Black and being White have specific
meaning. That the school and community also see newcomers to ESL programs as "good" students, unlike Americanized Hmong, can only be understood in light of a Hmong community that struggled hard to get their families
here, as well as the ongoing impact of the families on the students' lives.
Moreover, that Hmong students, particularly those who are ideologically
"blackened," are distanced from students of East Asian ancestry can, once
again, only be understood in light of the racial hierarchy in the United States
and the ways in which some Asian-American students are rendered "model
minorities" and positioned as honorary "Whites." And that all this plays out
differently for young men and women is only fully comprehended when
one considers an economy that allows and encourages women to earn
money and the fact that Hmong traditional culture embodies a particular
form of patriarchy. Indeed, Stacey Lee handles this range of complicated
and knotty theoretical and empirical issues exceptionally well, and offers a
most provocative piece of scholarship.

We have relatively few studies on students of Asian ancestry in United
States schools, but Lee has been at the forefront of work in this area. In
this volume she offers not only a powerful portrait of how such students
go to school—in this case a "good" school—but also the ways in which
the Hmong are being woven and yet simultaneously weaving themselves
into the American class and racial mosaic.

Lois Weis
University at Buffalo
State University of New York

REFERENCES

Centrie, C. (2004). *Identity formation of Vietnamese immigrant youth in an American high school.* New York: LFB Scholarly Publishing.

Dimitriadis, G. (2003). *Friendship, cliques and gangs: Young Black men coming of age in urban America.* New York: Teachers College Press.

Everhart, R. (1983). *Reading, writing and resistance.* Boston: Routledge and Keagan Paul.

Fine, M. (1991). *Framing dropouts: Notes on the politics of an urban public school.* Albany: State University of New York Press.

Foley, D. (1990). *Learning capitalist culture: Deep in the heart of Texas.* Philadelphia: University of Pennsylvania Press.

Lee, S. (1996). *Unraveling the "model minority" stereotype: Listening to Asian youth.* New York: Teachers College Press.

Luttrell, W. (1997). *Schoolsmart and motherwise: Working-class women's identity and schooling.* New York: Routledge.

Ogbu, J. (1974). *The next generation.* New York: Academic Press.

Proweller, A. (1998). *Constructing female identities: Meaning making in an upper middle class youth culture.* Albany: State University of New York Press.

Solomon, P. (1992). *Black resistance in high school.* Albany: State University of New York Press.

Valenzuela, A. (1999). *Subtractive schooling: U.S.-Mexican youth and the politics of caring.* Albany: State University of New York Press.

Weis, L. (1990). *Working class without work: High school students in a de-industrializing economy.* New York: Routledge.

Weis, L. (2004). *Class reunion: The remaking of the American White working class.* New York: Routledge.

Weis, L., & Fine, M. (2004). *Working method: Research and social justice.* New York: Routledge.

Wexler, P. (1987). *Social analysis of education.* New York: Routledge.

Willis, P. (1977). *Learning to labour: How working class kids get working class jobs.* Westmead, UK: Saxon House Press.

Acknowledgments

I have been fortunate to have the support and assistance of many through-out the course of this project, and I would like to take the time now to extend my appreciation to all of you. Graduate and undergraduate students at the University of Wisconsin-Madison raised important questions that helped me to sort out my ideas. Numerous project assistants over the years have provided important support, and I could not have completed this manuscript without them. Tara Affolter, Natalie Becker, Bic Ngo, Gilbert Park, Sophia Ward, and Anjela Wong transcribed tapes, tracked down citations, and/or provided computer assistance. Special thanks to Mary Jo Gessler for helping me get the manuscript off. Susan Liddicoat at Teachers College Press did another meticulous editing job, and encouraged me to write a reader-friendly book. I am indebted to Mai Zong Vue, Nou Yang, Ying Vang, Nicole Yang and See Vang for helping me to better understand the diverse experiences of Hmong Americans. Thank you to Mark Pfeifer at the Hmong Cultural Center in St. Paul for helping me navigate the 2000 census data on Hmong in the United States. Mike Olneck, Terrie Epstein, Lois Weis, Donna Deyhle, Xue Rong, Niobe Way, Michelle Fine, Kevin Kumashiro, Joy Lei, Lisa Loutzenheiser, Angelina Castagno, and Sabina Vaught read and commented on various chapters of the manuscript, and all raised important questions that helped to shape the final version. Thanks to the anonymous reviewers for providing insightful comments on an early draft of the manuscript. Thanks to family, friends and colleagues for listening to me talk—and talk—about this research and for offering important feedback. Special thanks to Lisa Konoplisky for reading all of my work, listening to me work out my ideas, and generally keeping me afloat. Lisa, Rubble, Streakie, Tango, Hannah, and Greenie help me to embrace life outside of the academy. Thank you to the faculty and staff at University Heights High School for welcoming me into their offices and classrooms. Finally, I want to express my deep appreciation to the Hmong American youth at University Heights High School for sharing their stories and letting me into their lives.

Becoming Racialized Americans

Toua was asking people to sign her memory book at lunch, and when she saw me, she asked me to sign, too. She explained that she is not getting a yearbook because of the expense. As I flipped through Toua's memory book, I found the following written in the back: "What is Hmong? When I am at a Hmong New Year I know. Until I speak to an elder, born and raised on rice and ginger root back in the mountains of Laos. Then it is that I am too American speaking in my broken tones and childlike mimicry. But at school it is different, at school I am Hmong. I swim in a sea of people: White, Black, Hispanic, French, English, Jamaican, Chinese, Korean. 'What are you?' They ask me. 'I am Hmong.' No flinching or hesitation . . ." Toua said that she was not sure, but she thinks it was written by "some guy in St. Paul." She explained that it had become popular among Hmong teens because it captured the experiences of young Hmong people in the United States. When I asked her to elaborate, she asserted that Hmong kids all have to deal with intergenerational conflict over culture and with being "minorities" in the United States.

Field note, 5/24/99

This book explores the way a group of first- and second-generation Southeast Asian Americans, specifically Hmong American high school students, create their identities as "new Americans." As the field note at the beginning of this chapter suggests, the process of identity formation is a particularly complex one for immigrant youth who must navigate various and often competing messages regarding identity. Like other youth from immigrant families, the Hmong American students in my study must negotiate cultural differences within a social context of unequal power relations. As youth of color, they must also negotiate dominant messages regarding race that position them in subordinate positions in society. In this book I will argue that race occupies the central role in Hmong American student experiences and significantly affects their understanding of what it means to be Hmong in the United States.

Like their counterparts from other immigrant groups, the Hmong American students in this book gather much of their information regarding

"America" and "being American" through their negotiation of schooling. Messages about race are central to what the children of immigrants learn in our schools (S. Lee, 1996; Lei, 2001; Olsen, 1997). Lessons about race—what is said as well as what is not said—saturate school policies, curricula, and interactions with peers and teachers. Non-White immigrant youth discover that they must negotiate their identities within a racial hierarchy where Whites are positioned at the top. Furthermore, they learn that there is a stigma attached to being non-White and immigrant (Olsen, 1997; Park, 1997; Valenzuela, 1999).

The central concern of this book is the way Hmong American youth create their identities in the context of the school and in response to their school experiences (e.g., interracial peer relationships, extracurricular participation, relationships with teachers, and academic achievement). In addition to examining the impact of school experiences on Hmong American identities, the book considers the way their experiences in the larger society, and in their ethnic community influence their identities.

As first- and second-generation Southeast Asian American youth from working-class and poor families, the Hmong American students in my study have to negotiate the racial hegemony of the school and the larger U.S. society. Although they are racial outsiders at the school, they are not simply passive victims of racism. Hmong American expressions of identity are constrained and limited by racial barriers, but ultimately Hmong American identities are not fully determined by racism. While schools are institutions where ideas about race and racial inequality are reproduced, they are also places of potential resistance. This book pays particular attention to Hmong American students' encounters with racism, their responses to their subordinate positions in school and in the larger American society, and the way Hmong American youth create their identities on the margins of the school. Significantly, the students do not respond to the subordination in uniform ways, but construct various ways of "being Hmong" at the school. In exploring the various ways that the Hmong American youth create their identities, this book uncovers expressions of identities that emerge because of and despite the inequalities at the school and in the larger society (Tsing, 1993).

While much has been written about the experiences of low-income immigrants of color who attend poorly funded schools with bad reputations (e.g., Olsen, 1997; Valenzuela, 1999; Zhou & Bankston, 1998), little has been written about the experiences of immigrants of color in "good" schools. The Hmong American youth in my study attended a relatively well-funded school with a reputation for academic excellence. While many immigrant youth of color attend racially segregated schools, the students in my study attend a school with a racially and economically diverse student population.

Despite the school's reputation for academic excellence, many Hmong American students fell through the cracks of the school. I will argue that the school's culture (e.g., curriculum, policies, staff, tacit cultural norms, etc.) reflected, perpetuated, and privileged White, middle-class cultural norms. In particular, I will argue that teachers' definitions of "good" students reveal White, middle-class cultural norms. Because the culture of the school reflects and serves White middle-class students Hmong American students' experiences remain largely unseen and Hmong American students' needs are largely unmet. In short, Hmong American students were excluded and alienated on the basis of race, culture, and class. The experiences of the Hmong American students in this study raise important questions regarding the characteristics of a "good" school.

RACE AND ASIAN AMERICAN IMMIGRANTS

As Asian immigrants and their children enter the United States they encounter a society in which race has always been and continues to be central to the national discourse on identity (Feagin, 2000; Omi & Winant, 1994; Takagi, 1992; Winant, 2001). Race and racism are central to the foundation of U.S. institutions (Bell, 1992; Crenshaw et al., 1995; Gotanda, 1995). While immigrants may imagine an idealized America that is open and free, what they find is a society where race and racism structure identities, experiences, and opportunities. Through their encounters with the dominant society, Asian American immigrants undergo a process of racialization and become racialized. That is, they become racial minorities.

In the United States discussions of race generally focus on Whites and Blacks. Within this largely White and Black dichotomy that surrounds the U.S. conversation on race, whiteness is constructed as the norm and blackness is constructed as the ultimate other (Dyer, 1993; Feagin, 2000; Frankenberg, 1993; Ong, 2003). Feagin (2000) writes, "The racist continuum runs from white to black, from 'civilized' whites to 'uncivilized' blacks, from high intelligence to low intelligence, from privilege and desirability to lack of privilege and undesirability" (p. 210). Within this racist discourse ideas regarding race and class are conflated. Whiteness is associated with economic self-sufficiency, independence, and self-discipline, while blackness is associated with welfare dependency, failure, and depravity. In other words, whiteness and middle class-ness are seen as being synonymous and blackness and poverty are seen as being synonymous, further naturalizing the Black-and-White thinking on race within a normative economic system.

Despite the enormous power that race has on the lives of all people in the United States, it is important to remember that race is a social construction. That is, race and racial categories are not based on biology, but on social ideas. The socially constructed nature of race and racial categories can be seen in the struggle for whiteness (Ignatiev, 1995; Roediger, 1991; Waters, 1999; Winant, 2001). During the 19th century, for example, European immigrants were initially identified as being distinct from White residents in the United States (i.e., WASPs) and from Blacks and non-White immigrants. Winant (2001) asserts that European immigrants competed to achieve economic stability and categorization as Whites, "an achievement that could only be gained at the expense of blacks" (p. 152).

Whiteness is both invisible and ubiquitous in defining "American-ness." Specifically, whiteness is associated with all that is ostensibly good about America and "being American." Blackness, by contrast, is associated with all that is ostensibly bad about America and being American. Thus, to be considered "good" immigrants must aspire to and show the likelihood of achieving middle-class status and in other ways assimilate to the dominant White culture. Poor immigrants who want to achieve upward mobility in mainstream American society often interpret the racial conditions to mean that they must simultaneously embrace whiteness and reject blackness (Islam, 2000; Park, 1997; Waters, 1999). Embracing whiteness, however, does not mean that the status of whiteness is in fact available to non-Whites.

While whiteness and blackness are constructed as the two faces of America, Asians and Asian Americans have historically been situated as perpetual foreigners (Lowe, 1996; Tuan, 1998). Asian Americans have often been characterized as being unable or unwilling to assimilate into American culture and society. During the 19th and 20th centuries the dominant perception that the Chinese culture prevented Chinese immigrants from ever assimilating into the American culture contributed to the passing of exclusion acts that aimed at excluding the entry of all Chinese immigrants into the United States (Chan, 1991; Jaret, 1999; Takaki, 1989). Lowe (1996) elaborates on the construction of Asian American immigrants as being outside the category of citizen when she writes, "In the last century and a half, the American *citizen* has been defined over and against the Asian *immigrant*, legally, economically, and culturally" (p. 4). In other words, Lowe argues that Asian immigrants have been marginalized as permanent outsiders in the United States.

As permanent outsiders, Asian Americans are forever associated with their country of origin. While the descendents of European immigrants have become accepted as authentic Americans, Asian Americans are always considered to be foreigners regardless of the number of generations their families have been in the United States. In her research on multiple-generation Asian Americans, for example, Tuan (1998) discovered that her subjects were identified as "forever foreigners" and denied the opportunity to identify solely as Americans. In comparing the situation of Asian Americans with White Americans, Frank Wu (2002) writes,

> Historically, Chinese immigrants and Irish immigrants arrived at about the same time and competed against one another in the same endeavors and geographic areas. But Chinese Americans have not been accepted in the same manner as Irish Americans. (p. 123)

Identified as perpetual foreigners, Asian Americans' patriotism and loyalty to the United States are always in question. One indication that Asian Americans continue to be viewed as foreigners (i.e., not Americans) is that attitudes toward Asian Americans are highly influenced by international relations between the United States and Asian countries (Lowe, 1996; Nakayama, 1994; Wu, 2002). When international relations with Asian countries are tense, Asian Americans are viewed suspiciously as potential threats to national security. Similarly, during times of domestic crisis Asian Americans are often seen as a "yellow peril" poised to take away jobs from "real Americans" (Lowe, 1996).

Although Asian Americans have been cast as perpetual foreigners and therefore not American, Asian American experiences have historically been influenced by the Black-and-White thinking about race (Feagin, 2000; Loewen, 1971; Okihiro, 1994; Wu, 2002). Depending on the historical period, Asian Americans have been likened to Blacks or likened to Whites (Loewen, 1971; Okihiro, 1994; Takaki, 1989). Early Chinese immigrants, for example, were likened to Blacks (Takaki, 1989). During the 1960s the stereotype of Asian Americans as hard-working and successful "model minorities" emerged and Asian Americans were thereby likened to Whites. According to the model minority rhetoric, the success of Asian Americans proves that the United States is an open society free of racial bias and inequality (S. Lee, 1996; Osajima, 1988; Tuan, 1998).

Within the model minority rhetoric, Asian Americans are represented as "good" minorities and African Americans are represented as "bad" minorities. Here, the achievements of Asian Americans are used to discipline African Americans. As model minorities, Asian Americans achieved the status of "honorary Whites" (Tuan, 1998). Again, it is important to point out that the honorary whiteness of Asian Americans was granted at the expense of Blacks (Winant, 2001). It is also significant that as "honorary

Whites," Asian Americans do not have the actual privileges associated with "real" whiteness.

Although the model minority stereotype may appear to signal that Asian Americans gained acceptance as Americans, the perpetual foreigner and model minority stereotypes coexist and reinforce each other (R. Lee, 1999; Okihiro, 1994). In discussing the relationship between these two stereotypes, Robert Lee (1999) writes:

> The Asian American model minority is thus a simulacrum of both an imaginary Asian tradition from which it is wishfully constructed and an American culture for which it serves as a nostalgic mirror. The model minority can operate as the paragon of conservative virtues that all Americans should emulate only if Asian Americans remain *like* "us" but utterly are *not* "us." (p. 183)

Thus, whether likened to Whites or Blacks, Asian Americans are ultimately used to serve the interest of whiteness (Feagin, 2000).

Ong (1999) argues that the Black-and-White discourse on race frames the way recent non-White immigrants are viewed by the dominant society. Specifically, she asserts that immigrant groups are either ideologically whitened or blackened depending on their economic standing. In her ethnographic research, Ong (1999) observed that middle- and upper-middle-class Chinese immigrants have been ideologically whitened in the dominant imagination and that lower-income Southeast Asian refugees have been ideologically blackened in the dominant imagination.

The "ideological whitening" of middle-class East Asian immigrants that Ong describes is similar to the characterization of Asian Americans as "model minorities." Here, the economic success of East Asian immigrants leads to their status as "honorary whites" (Tuan, 1998). By contrast, Hmong, Lao, and Cambodian refugees have been blackened in the dominant imagination because of the high rates of poverty within their communities. Ong (2003) elaborates that the very category of *refugee* evokes images of destitute victims in need of shelter. While refugees may initially be met with sympathy, Ong (1999, 2003) argues that refugees who are unable to quickly become self-sufficient are perceived to be economic burdens on society. Ong's work demonstrates that race and class work together in the racialization of Asian immigrants. Thus, poor and working-class Asian immigrants and refugees are seen as Americanizing in "bad ways," and middle-class Asian immigrants are seen as Americanizing in "good ways."

While Asian American immigrants are seen as Americanizing and becoming Americanized, they are never accepted as authentic Americans. Asian immigrant cultures mark Asian Americans as different and in essence un-American. While success may in some ways "whiten" middle-class Asian Americans, it does not grant Asian Americans the status of whiteness. While I would agree with Ong (1999) that lower-income Southeast Asians have been ideologically blackened in the dominant discourse, I would add that they also bear the stain of the perpetual foreigner (Tuan, 1998; Wu, 2002). Cast as perpetual foreigners, the problematic refugee is subject to deportation. The assumption regarding the foreignness of Southeast Asian refugees is reflected in policies that allow for the deportation of refugees (i.e., permanent residents who have not become naturalized citizens) who have been convicted of crimes (Sontag, 2003).

Recently anti-immigration activists have used the supposed cultural differences of immigrants to suggest that their presence is a threat to American culture and society. The Patriot Act is perhaps the most striking example of this anti-immigrant thinking. A focus on the presumed dangerous nature of immigrant cultures reflects what some scholars refer to as cultural racism or racism without race (Appiah, 1996; Balibar, 1992; Gilroy, 1990; Winant, 2001). Within the rhetoric of cultural racism, culture functions as a stand in for race. Cultural racism rejects the notion of inherent biological differences (Balibar, 1992; Winant, 2001). However, Balibar (1992) points out that "culture can also function like a nature, and it can in particular function as a way of locking individuals and groups a priori into a genealogy, into a determination that is immutable and intangible in origin" (p. 22). Thus, culture is understood to be fixed and static, not fluid and in process. It is worth noting that the notion of cultural difference has been used to debase and control colonized peoples (Smith, 1999; Tsing, 1993). Because cultural racism avoids discussion of biological differences, it appeals to those who see themselves as nonracists. A focus on culture is in some ways consistent with the color-blind perspective that denies the significance of race.

The historical and contemporary constructions of Asian Americans as perpetual foreigners and the dominant Black-and-White discourse on race frame the experiences of newer Asian American immigrants, including the Hmong American youth in my study. I will argue that Hmong American students are identified as culturally different and therefore not American (i.e., foreign) or they are seen as Americanizing in bad and dangerous ways (i.e., blackened).

ASSIMILATION THEORIES RECONSIDERED

Much of the academic literature on immigrants in the United States has focused on issues related to cultural assimilation. Based on the experiences of European immigrants who entered the United States during the early part of the 20th century, straight-line assimilation theories predicted a linear path from foreigner/immigrant to mainstream American (Gordon, 1964; Park, 1950). According to this perspective there was one path to becoming American, and it required the rejection of native cultures in favor of the mainstream "American" culture (i.e., White, middle-class culture). The assumption was that ethnic identity would ultimately become a choice for assimilated Americans. Cultural assimilation was understood to be a prerequisite for socioeconomic assimilation, social mobility, and the successful achievement of the American dream. Failure to assimilate into the dominant culture was understood to be problematic for both the immigrant and the larger society. According to this perspective, groups who fail to assimilate are a political, economic, and social threat to the country. Because cultural assimilation has been assumed to be in the best interest of immigrant groups and the larger society, public schools have long been charged with "Americanizing" immigrant students (Olneck, 2004). In fact, ideas about the importance of assimilation are at the heart of the popular "melting pot" metaphor. Through assimilation it is assumed that we will all become the same.

Because the Immigration Act of 1924 set nationality quotas for admission based on the U.S. population in 1890, most immigrants during the first major wave of immigration were of European descent. The Immigration Act of 1965 abolished the national origins quotas, thereby opening the doors to immigrants from Asia and Latin America. With the influx of post-1965 immigrants, there has been a renewed interest in immigrants, particularly their social, cultural, and economic adjustment. Much of the newer body of research criticizes straight-line assimilation theories for being ethnocentric. Some scholars, for example, charge that straight-line assimilation has never been an option for immigrants of color. Unlike the ancestors of European immigrants, who can choose whether or not to identify as ethnics, non-White ethnics have always found ethnic labels imposed on them by the dominant group (Espiritu, 1992; Tuan, 1998; Waters, 1990). While second-generation European Americans can choose to identify solely as Americans, researchers have found that multiple-generation Asian Americans are often not accepted as authentic Americans (Tuan, 1998). In short, a conflation of whiteness with American-ness has excluded Asian Americans from the category of American.

Some researchers have focused on the differences between post-1965 immigrants and earlier immigrants. Many current sociologists of immigration, for example, argue that the old assimilation theories are incapable of capturing the experiences of post-1965 immigrants who are more culturally, racially, and economically diverse than previous generations of immigrants (Gans, 1992; Portes & Rumbaut, 2001; Waldinger, 2001). Some predict that the combination of racism and changes in the economy that have resulted in fewer opportunities for less skilled immigrants will lead to a "second-generation decline" (Gans, 1992).

Others argue that the children of today's immigrants (i.e., the new second generation) will experience segmented assimilation (Portes & Rumbaut, 2001; Portes & Zhou, 1993; Zhou, 2001). These scholars have challenged assumptions regarding the benefits of cultural assimilation for all immigrants. In their description of the different paths of segmented assimilation, Portes and Zhou (1993) write:

> One of them replicates the time-honored portrayal of growing acculturation and parallel integration into the white middle-class; a second leads straight in the opposite direction to permanent poverty and assimilation into the underclass; still a third associates rapid economic advancement with deliberate preservation of the immigrant community's values and tight solidarity. (p. 82)

According to these scholars, only middle-class immigrants from highly educated backgrounds are well positioned to achieve assimilation into White middle-class society. The majority of working-class and poor immigrants of color, on the other hand, either assimilate into the underclass or achieve social mobility through the maintenance of distinct ethnic communities (Portes & Zhou, 1993; Zhou, 1997).

Zhou (1997) argues that the low socioeconomic status of many immigrant families puts their children at risk to the dangers of poor, urban America. Poor immigrant youth of color are characterized as being vulnerable to assimilation into the oppositional culture associated with urban youth of color (Portes & Zhou, 1993; Zhou, 1997; Zhou & Bankston, 1998). Youth who develop oppositional cultures reject education as a viable route to social mobility (Matute-Bianchi, 1986; Ogbu, 1987). Thus, this type of Americanization (i.e., assimilation into urban youth culture) is understood to be dangerous and problematic.

Much of this current research on immigrants suggests that ethnic communities can protect youth from urban influences. The maintenance of ethnic ties and ethnic identities is understood to be central to immigrant achievement (Gibson, 1988; Kao & Tienda, 1995; Portes & Rumbaut, 2001; Valenzuela, 1999; Zhou & Bankston, 1998). Social capital in the form that ethnic networks provides economic support for immigrants and reinforces parental authority in immigrant families (Portes & Rumbaut, 2001; Zhou & Bankston, 1998). For example, in their study of Vietnamese immigrants and their children, Zhou and Bankston (1998) found that the most successful Vietnamese immigrants possess significant social capital in the form of ties to the larger Vietnamese community.

According to the work on segmented assimilation, the most successful immigrants practice selective acculturation whereby immigrant parents and their children learn English and mainstream American norms
while preserving aspects of their native language and norms (Portes &
Rumbaut, 2001). In discussing the benefits of selective acculturation, Portes
and Rumbaut (2001) write:

> Children who learn the language and culture of their new country without
> losing those of the old have a much better understanding of their place in
> the world. They need not clash with their parents as often or feel embar-
> rassed by them because they are able to bridge the gap across generations
> and value their elders' traditions and goals. Selective acculturation forges
> an intergenerational alliance for successful adaptation that is absent among
> youths who have severed bonds with their past in the pursuit of acceptance
> by their native peers. (p. 274)

Research conducted by educational researchers also points to the value
of selective acculturation for mainstream success. In her ethnographic
study on Sikh immigrant students and their families, for example, Gibson
(1988) concluded that "accommodation and acculturation without assimilation" supports academic success. According to Gibson, the strategy of accommodation and acculturation without assimilation involves
conforming to certain rules of the dominant society and making certain
cultural adaptations while preserving the group's cultural identity. The
strength of this body of work is that it challenges the ethnocentric assumptions behind straight-line assimilation theories by demonstrating
the significance of ethnic communities and cultures in immigrant adaptation and achievement.

Like others who challenge straight-line assimilation theories, I am
interested in how immigrant and second-generation youth are transforming and re-creating their cultures in response to life in the United States.
I am particularly interested in how immigrants of color are responding to
messages about race. How do conditions of racism and discourses of race
shape opportunities and identities of immigrants of color? How do immigrants accommodate and resist the dominant culture?

While the research on segmented assimilation considers the role of
race and racism on the lives of immigrants of color, the literature does
not pay enough attention to the process of racialization that immigrants
must necessarily undergo; that is, the way race informs immigrant encounters with social institutions and shapes immigrant identities. For
example, while the segmented assimilation literature reveals the relationship between modes of adaptation and achievement, it does not focus
enough attention on the role of schools in the formation of youth iden-

tities. Although this literature provides a fairly clear picture of how youth are responding to school, it does not provide an in-depth understanding of how schools are treating them. Thus, it does not adequately address how schools contribute to the creation of oppositional identities among some youth of color from immigrant families. The failure to adequately examine the role of schools results in the implicit blaming of students for their academic resistance.

Educational researchers have focused on the continuing role that schools play in promoting a Eurocentric vision of America that excludes immigrant and American-born students of color (Olsen, 1997; Valenzuela, 1999). Despite the rhetoric about multiculturalism in many schools, many elementary and secondary teachers continue to rely on straight-line assimilation theories in interpreting the experiences of immigrant students in U.S. schools (S. Lee, 1996; Olsen, 1997). In an effort to assimilate immigrant and second-generation students, schools engage in a subtractive process whereby they strip students of their family's language and culture (Cummins, 1986; Gibson, 1988; Valenzuela, 1999). In her research on Mexican American high school students, Valenzuela (1999) argues that the academic problems experienced by many second-generation students "are themselves symptomatic of the ways that schooling is organized to subtract resources from them" (p. 5). From this perspective, the oppositional culture expressed by some students is a response to the actions of the school. Like other educational researchers, I am interested in focusing attention on the school. Specifically, I am interested in the role that school plays in shaping immigrant and second-generation students' identities and responses to life in the United States. What do schools teach immigrants about race? What do they teach immigrants about "America" and "being American"? In this book, I focus specifically on the experiences of Hmong American students.

THE HMONG IN THE UNITED STATES

The first Hmong arrived in the United States as refugees from Laos over 25 years ago. Originally an ethnic group from China, these Hmong had lived in Laos since the 18th century when they fled China because of ethnic persecution. As in China, the Hmong were viewed as ethnic outsiders in Laos. Religious differences between Lao Buddhists and Hmong animists contributed to the tensions between the groups (Faderman & Xiong, 1998). Central to traditional Hmong religious beliefs are ancestor worship and the practice of shamanism (G. Lee, 1996; Thao, 1999). Hmong made their livings in Laos as slash-and-burn farmers in remote mountain regions.

Hmong society was based on the patrilineal family. Life was organized around the extended family or clan, and members of a given clan are viewed as relatives (Donnelly, 1994; Faderman & Xiong, 1998).

During the Vietnam War Hmong soldiers served as U.S. allies in the "secret war" against communism in Laos. As early as 1959 the CIA recruited Hmong men to gather intelligence about North Vietnamese movement in Laos. In the 1960s the CIA recruited Hmong soldiers to fight communist forces. In return for their service, the Hmong were promised U.S. protection if the war was lost (Faderman & Xiong, 1998). Some of the most serious battles in Laos took place near Hmong villages, forcing Hmong villagers to flee for their lives. By the end of the war, boys as young as 10 years of age were recruited to fight. The Hmong suffered tremendous casualties, and in some villages there were few adult males alive at the war's end.

After the war, waves of Hmong refugees fled to Thailand, where they spent months and even years before being resettled. U.S. policy required Southeast Asian refugees, including Hmong refugees, to register with voluntary agencies that had contracts with the federal government to help refugees resettle and find sponsors. The sponsors helped to provide food, shelter, and general assistance to refugees. Approximately 60% of the sponsors were families, 25% were churches or other organized groups, and the rest were individuals (Chan, 1991). Federal policy encouraged the resettlement of Southeast Asian refugees around the country in order to minimize the burden on a single state and in order to encourage assimilation (Chan, 1991). The importance of extended families among Southeast Asians, however, led to significant secondary migration and the creation of concentrated Southeast Asian communities. In explaining the concentration of Hmong in Wisconsin, Hutchinson (1992) pointed to "federal policy to limit refugee resettlement in California, the prevalence of church-based sponsor groups, and the regrouping of Hmong clans" (p. 286). Approximately 130,000 Hmong refugees were resettled in the United States between the end of the war and 1996.

According to the 2000 census, there are 186,310 people who identify themselves as Hmong living in the United States (U.S. Census Bureau, 2000). Like other immigrant communities, the Hmong American community is young, with a median age of 16.1. The largest Hmong American communities are in California (65,095), Minnesota (41,800), and Wisconsin (33,791). It is worth noting that the Hmong American community believes that the official census numbers reflect an undercount. Members of the Hmong American community cite language and cultural barriers as probable causes for this. In discussing this issue, Pfeifer and Lee (2004) write, "It seems very plausible that the 2000 Census data that were collected from persons of Hmong origin were at least somewhat skewed to the proportion of the population that is more acculturated into mainstream American culture in terms of education, English language ability and other socioeconomic variables" (p. 3). Based on figures given by Hmong community leaders and service organizations, the Hmong American community estimates that the total Hmong population in the United States in 2000 was 283,239 (Hmong National Development Inc., www.hndlink.org).

Secondary migration has led to significant growth in the Hmong population in the Midwest. Thus, while the population of Hmong in California grew 38% since the 1990 census, the Hmong population in Minnesota grew 135%, and the Hmong population in Wisconsin grew 99% (Pfeifer & Lee, 2004). In California the Hmong population is concentrated around Fresno, and in Minnesota around St. Paul and Minneapolis. In contrast to the Hmong American populations in California and Minnesota, the Hmong American population in Wisconsin is distributed across several cities. Other states with significant Hmong populations include North Carolina, Michigan, Colorado, Oregon, Georgia, Washington, Massachusetts, Kansas, Rhode Island, Pennsylvania, Oklahoma, and South Carolina.

Despite the fact that Hmong immigrants/refugees have been in the United States for over 25 years, many people in this country are largely unaware of who they are or why they are here. Not long ago I was asked to participate in a documentary on immigrant families in U.S. schools. When the documentary filmmaker found out that I was currently doing research on Hmong students I was asked whether I could focus on "a more well-known group, like the Chinese." In my work as a professor at the University of Wisconsin-Madison, I have been struck by how little many of the undergraduate students from Wisconsin know about why the Hmong are in the United States, although this state has the third-largest population of people of Hmong descent. In part, the invisibility of the Hmong is related to their being U.S. allies in a secret war. The invisibility of the Hmong is also related to the silence surrounding the Hmong in public school curricula. Those people who do know something about the Hmong have generally gathered their information from popular accounts that tend to stereotype Hmong culture.

Early scholarly and popular accounts of Hmong refugees emphasized the differences between Hmong culture and mainstream American culture. Hmong culture was described as rural, preliterate, patriarchal, clannish, and traditional. These comparisons served to highlight the supposedly exotic nature of Hmong culture and to make "normal" mainstream American culture. Central to the descriptions of Hmong refugees was an implicit understanding that Hmong culture was somehow static and largely untouched by time (e.g., Beck, 1994; Fass, 1991; Rumbaut & Ima, 1988;

Sherman, 1988). In other words, Hmong culture was understood to be primitive and unchanged by history. The problem with this framework is that it does not recognize that Hmong culture has always been responsive to social conditions, first in China, then in Laos, and now in the United States (Dunnigan, 1986; Fish, 1991; Hendricks, 1986). In recent history, the Hmong have transformed their culture in response to war, migration, life in refugee camps, and resettlement in the United States. There are, for example, Hmong living in the United States, China, and Southeast Asia who have converted to Christianity (G. Lee, 1996; Thao, 1999). Some converts to Christianity have blended their new beliefs with traditional Hmong religious beliefs (Thao, 1999).

While Hmong culture is described as being largely frozen in time, mainstream American culture is implicitly characterized as progressive, modern, individualistic, and advanced. In describing the Hmong, one policy analyst asserted, "This country has rarely, if ever, welcomed a group of immigrants so culturally distant from the native social and economic mainstream" (Fass, 1991, p. 1). According to much of the popular and academic literature, the differences between Hmong culture and mainstream American culture are understood to be at the root of many of the social and economic problems (e.g., welfare dependence, high school dropout rates) that Hmong refugees face in the United States. For example, cultural barriers have been identified as the reason behind the high dropout rates among Hmong refugee students in middle and high school (Cohn, 1986; Goldstein, 1985). Hmong girls, in particular, experienced high dropout rates, which were traced back to the Hmong cultural practices of early marriage and early childrearing (Goldstein, 1985; Rumbaut & Ima, 1988; Walker-Moffat, 1995; see also chapter 4, this volume).

By focusing solely on the Hmong culture, the dominant culture implicitly located the problem within the group. Although an understanding of cultural issues is important, an exclusive focus on culture denies the existence of economic, racial, and other structural barriers that Hmong immigrants/refugees face. The singular attention on culture conceals the impact of race and racism on the Hmong American community and leaves the assumptions of the dominant culture unchallenged. In fact, much of the focus on Hmong culture reflects the cultural racism of the dominant group. Hmong culture is implicitly understood to be inferior to mainstream American culture and ultimately threatening to the fabric of U.S. society.

The popular press, in particular, has subjected Hmong immigrants and Hmong culture to the kind of racist characterizations that African Americans have long experienced. Hmong immigrants/refugees, for example, have been characterized as deficient and unable to take advantage of the opportunities in the United States (Sherman, 1988). In an *Atlantic Monthly* article, Hmong immigrants were described as a threat to the middle-class American dream. According to the author, Hmong immigrants brought gangs, teen pregnancy, and welfare dependency to a previously idyllic setting (Beck, 1994). To borrow a phrase from Ong (1999), Hmong Americans have been "ideologically blackened" in much of the early scholarly and popular work on the Hmong. Like African Americans, Hmong Americans were characterized as culturally, intellectually, and morally inferior to Whites.

Hmong Americans are well aware of how they are characterized by the dominant society and have gone to considerable efforts to improve their position in U.S. society and to improve their public image. In fact, many within the Hmong American community now appear to define success in mainstream American ways. Status within the Hmong community, for example, is now linked to economic success (Koltyk, 1998).

Despite social, cultural, economic, and racial barriers, many Hmong Americans have been able to successfully adapt to life in the United States. There are Hmong Americans who serve on school boards in Wisconsin. Two Hmong Americans serve as state legislators in Minnesota. In addition to these individual successes, there is evidence that the Hmong population as a whole has made progress. According to the 2000 census, Hmong Americans have made gains in educational attainment, household income levels, and homeownership (Pfeifer & Lee, 2004). While 62% of Hmong families were below the poverty level in 1990, 34.8% of Hmong families were below the poverty level in 2000. In 2000, 38.74% lived in owner occupied housing, up from 13% in 1990. (Author's note: economic data, such as income and poverty levels, are from U.S. Census Bureau, 2000b; educational attainment data from U.S. Census Bureau, 2000c). A growing number of Hmong American men and women have gone on to pursue higher education (Fass, 1991; Lee 1997; Ngo, 2000). According to the 2000 census, 5.9% of the U.S. Hmong population 25 years and over have earned a bachelor's degree.

The ability of Hmong Americans to adapt to life in the United States appears to be due in part to their history as minorities in China and Laos. As such, the Hmong have always had to respond and adapt to dominant conditions to survive as a distinct ethnic group. Writing about the early Hmong refugees in San Diego, Scott (1982) stated, "The Hmong are accustomed to adversity, and in the past they have always managed to survive. Given time, that will happen here " (p. 154). Scott's prediction appears to come true for many Hmong in the United States.

While some members of the Hmong American community have achieved mainstream success, many others continue to face formidable barriers to mobility. Some observers have suggested that the poverty rates within the Hmong American community may be higher than indicated in the 2000 census, since illiterate and poor persons are those most likely to have been left out of the official census count (Vang, 2004). Many elderly and disabled Hmong adults are struggling to survive in the post-welfare reform era. The federal Welfare Reform Act, passed in 1996, called for the termination of Supplemental Security Income (SSI) for non-citizens except for refugees, who are allowed seven years of SSI. Age, disability, and language barriers, however, make it difficult for many of the elderly and disabled to pass the U.S. citizenship test requirements. In addition to the hardships faced by elderly and disabled Hmong, there is also growing evidence that some second-generation Hmong youth are becoming disillusioned with life in the United States (Thao, 1999).

As I make final revisions to this manuscript in 2004, Hmong American communities around the country are preparing for the influx of new Hmong refugees. In December of 2003 the United States announced that approximately 15,000 new Hmong refugees who have been living at the Wat Thamkrabok refugee camp in Thailand would be allowed to settle in the United States (Mydans, 2004). Included in this group of new refugees are adults who fled the communist takeover of Laos back in 1975 and young people who have lived their entire lives in the camps. Hmong Americans have expressed relief at the U.S. decision to accept new refugees, noting that the Hmong population in Laos is still regularly persecuted for having sided with the United States during the Vietnam War. Like the previous waves of Hmong refugees, the newcomers will face considerable cultural differences, racism, and economic barriers to their adjustment to life in the United States. These new refugees, however, will have the benefit of being welcomed by established Hmong American communities. In Wisconsin, for example, the Hmong Resettlement Task Force will be headed by a Hmong woman who is identified as the first Hmong school principal in the United States.

IN THE FIELD

This book is based on 1½ years of ethnographic research (January 1999–June 2000) on Hmong American students at a public school I call University Heights High School (UHS). The primary means of data collection were participant observation of Hmong American students in the high school (e.g., during class, lunch periods, study hall, and extracurricular activities) and semistructured interviews with Hmong American students and school staff. Semistructured interviews lasted from 1 to 3 hours and were taped when possible. I also examined school documents (e.g., yearbooks, student handbooks, club flyers) and observed Hmong parents at meetings organized by the school district. Although my primary research site was UHS, I borrowed the insights of Marcus (1995) regarding the importance of conducting multisited ethnography. Thus, in addition to fieldwork at UHS, I conducted participant observation at local Hmong community events, and researched Internet sites popular among Hmong American youth.

In many places in the book I provide verbatim quotes from interviews and describe individuals in great detail, but in other places I speak more generally about a group in an effort to protect the identity of individuals who revealed sensitive information that they did not want to be traced back to them.

University Heights High School

University Heights High School is located in what I call Lakeview, a midsized city in Wisconsin. Lakeview has a national reputation for being a socially and politically liberal city. The city has been recognized by numerous national polls and magazines for being a good place to live. According to the 2000 census, the racial makeup of Lakeview is 82% White, 5.8% African American, and 5.8% Asian. Forty-eight percent of the adults over 25 years of age have a college education, and 93% of adults over 25 have graduated from high school.

The Lakeview school district has been named one of the finest in the country by several national magazines. In the 1998–99 academic year, the annual expenditure per pupil in the Lakeview School District was $9,616. University Heights High is one of four comprehensive high schools in the district. As noted earlier, the school enjoys an excellent academic reputation in the city and throughout the state, and in 1985 UHS was awarded a "School of Excellence Award" by the U.S. Department of Education. The high school is located in a predominately White, middle- to upper-middle-class residential neighborhood. Within the city of Lakeview, this neighborhood is known as the home of the city's educated elite. Surrounding the UHS neighborhood are other middle- and upper-middle-class neighborhoods that feed students into UHS. In addition to drawing students from these neighborhoods, UHS draws students from the south side of the city, where lower-income housing is available. Most of the Hmong American students at UHS live on the Southside, where their neighbors are other lower-income people of color.

During the 1999–2000 academic year UHS enrolled 2023 students, with 29% of these students classified as students of color and 14% identified as receiving free or reduced-price lunch. Students of Asian descent represent 10% of the student population (206 students). Since UHS and the school district lump all students of Asian descent into one category as "Asians," it was difficult to get an exact count of the Hmong American students. According to estimates made by the various school staff, there were 54 Hmong American students enrolled at UHS during the 1998–99 school year and approximately 65 Hmong students enrolled during the 1999–2000 academic year.

Hmong is the first language in the homes of all of the Hmong American students at UHS, and most students' parents speak limited English. Most of the Hmong American students are from low-income families and receive free or reduced-price lunch. As noted earlier, most live in low-income housing in the poorer sections of the city, where lower-income African American and Latino families also live. Hmong American students reported that their parents worked in low-skilled jobs and/or received public assistance. Many families grow vegetables to sell at one of the many local farmers' markets. Two Hmong American students reported that their parents had recently bought their own homes, which suggests that some Hmong American families in Lakeview are moving out of poverty into the middle class.

Most Hmong American students at UHS were born in the United States and are therefore members of the second generation. Most of these students have been mainstreamed and do not have official connections to the English as a Second Language Department (ESL) at the school. There is also a smaller population of 1.5-generation Hmong American students at UHS who have been in the United States for three to eight years. The majority of these students are enrolled in the school's ESL program for at least a portion of their high school careers.

"You're Not Hmong, Are You? You're Chinese."

As in all ethnographic research, the identity of the researcher influenced the research process. With few exceptions, Hmong American students at UHS were acutely aware of issues of identity, and their perceptions of me affected our relationships. Students typically used ethnicity, race, gender, age, generation, and marital status to situate others. In my first encounters with Hmong students I was typically asked the following: "Are you Hmong?" "Where were you born?" "Are you married?" As a third-generation Chinese American woman, I share a panethnic/racial label with the Hmong students that helped to pave the way for initial conversations, but since I'm not Hmong I was still an ethnic outsider. By keeping the students' secrets, remaining nonjudgmental, and sharing bits of my own identity and history, I was eventually able to gain the confidence of a range of students. In an effort to determine my trustworthiness, some of my informants asked me about my Chinese cultural background before revealing aspects of their culture. When I told them that I spoke Chinese like a young child a few of the students laughed in appreciation. When they learned that I was in my mid-thirties and did not have a husband they concluded that I was "Americanized." For some students, my "Americanized" identity was seen as a positive thing, but for others it was seen as problematic. I generally had an easier time developing rapport with girls than I did with boys, a fact that I attribute to the relatively gender-segregated nature of Hmong culture.

In her research on Hmong immigrants in Wisconsin, Koltyk (1998) discovered that most Hmong go to great efforts to protect their culture from the gaze of outsiders. Koltyk (1998) explains, "As the Hmong have learned that aspects of their culture seem primitive or offensive to many Americans, they have become reluctant to talk to outsiders about them" (p. 14). Similarly, many of my informants would switch to speak in Hmong when discussing potentially sensitive topics (e.g., marriage, funerals). Girls who were married were careful to hide their marital status from school officials for fear of moral and sometimes legal judgment. Two of my primary informants did not disclose their marital status to me for several months.

Of course, my identity also influenced the way I initially saw the students. I am the granddaughter and great-granddaughter of Chinese American immigrants. My paternal grandparents were merchants in Boston's Chinatown, and my maternal grandparents were merchants in the Mississippi Delta. I grew up in a predominately White, upper-middle-class suburb in Southern California. As I listened to the stories of the Hmong American students and observed their actions, I often found myself comparing their experiences to my family's experiences. I was, for example, immediately struck by the fact that most of the Hmong American students in my study have Hmong first names. By contrast, most of the Chinese Americans I know from my parents' generation have European first names. They were given Chinese names as well, but these were either middle names or private family names. Even my paternal and maternal grandparents took European-sounding first names. It wasn't until I became acquainted with the Hmong youth at UHS that I fully appreciated my family's accommodation to the dominant culture. As I thought about my family, I also realized that while there were many moments of accommodation, there were also moments of resistance. My paternal grandmother, for example, insisted that her American-born children speak to her in Chinese. My newly found understanding of my family's adaptations led me to ask, how are Hmong Americans accommodating and resisting the dominant culture?

While the Hmong American students were the focus of my study, I also interviewed and observed teachers, counselors, administrators, and other adults at the school. Upon first meeting me, several UHS staff assumed that I was a graduate student and they welcomed me as a type of student. When I told these individuals that I taught at the University of Wisconsin, some became more guarded in my presence, while others saw me as a potential resource. A few teachers asked to see samples of my previous academic writing. Other UHS staff focused on my racial and ethnic identity. Several UHS staff asked me whether or not I was Hmong. One person appeared visibly relieved when she learned that I was not Hmong. Interestingly, this individual had been hesitant to answer my questions until she found out my ethnicity. Another began to sing the praises of "East Asians" upon learning that I am Chinese American.

I share this information about the impact of my identities on the research process in order to illustrate the constructed nature of ethnographic work. My experiences provide further support for the argument that researchers must negotiate the ways they are racialized by research participants (Twine, 2000). I also share the information because it provides a glimpse into how identities operated at UHS. At UHS, as in the larger society, identities and perceptions of identities structure social encounters. Throughout the book I will share information about my identity and the research process when it provides insight into the bigger picture of Hmong American identity formation at UHS.

A Note on the Politics of Research

Scholars from various disciplines and political perspectives have raised important concerns regarding the ethical and political issues surrounding ethnographic representation (e.g., Abu-Lughod, 1991; Clifford & Marcus, 1986; Fine, 1994; Fine & Weis, 1998; Fordham, 1996; Loutzenheiser, 2001; Smith, 1999; Stacey, 1988; Tillman, 2002; Twine, 2000). I agree with sociologist France Twine (2000) when she writes, "The issue of representation seems to be a particularly agonizing and complicated one for those researching communities vulnerable due to racial and ethnic inequalities" (p. 23).

I began this project well aware of how Hmong refugees in the United States have been essentialized and exoticized by journalists and academics, and I do not want my work to further stereotype Hmong Americans. I want to be clear that my work should not be viewed as a comprehensive account of Hmong or Hmong American culture. In fact, I doubt a single comprehensive account of Hmong American culture is possible. Although my goal is not to add to the fixed, static, rigid, and essentialized portraits of Hmong Americans, I recognize that by engaging in any description of

Hmong American youth and their culture I run the risk of doing just that. In an effort to counter essentialized representations of Hmong American youth, I have attempted to emphasize the internal diversity of the group. Through the stories of individual Hmong American youth, I will illustrate the various ways they respond to their marginalization within the United States. Gender and generation are just two of the factors which shape Hmong American identities and responses to life in the United States.

Because I do not want to contribute to narratives that position Hmong Americans as the "other," I have struggled over how to represent issues that may seem strange to people outside of the Hmong American community. At the same time, however, I cannot ignore or deny what I observed. In the ethnographic tradition, I have tried to get at how my participants, particularly the Hmong American youth, make sense of what they do (Erickson, 1986).

Because it is my goal to highlight the complexity of Hmong American experiences, I will convey material shared by students that may be considered private by certain members of the Hmong American community. I am aware of this possibility, given that the Hmong American community has worked, like other immigrant communities, to establish a positive public image within the dominant culture. While I appreciate and respect this desire for privacy, I hope to share stories that communicate the challenges of living as a subordinate group within a racialized society. For example, in discussing girls who hide their married status I hope to portray the difficult position of girls who must negotiate two often competing social contexts.

Throughout the book I have attempted to emphasize the constructed nature of Hmong American identities. One of my primary goals in this book is to demonstrate the way racism informs and constrains identity options. In this way, I see my work as being as much about Hmong American youth as it is about the White institution under which they struggle. In a broader sense, this is a story of how one group of low-income immigrant youth of color struggle to become American under hegemonic racial conditions. I hope that as readers learn about Hmong American youth they will also learn about our schools.

ROAD MAP FOR THE BOOK

In this chapter I have outlined the research questions and literatures that drive this work, and have discussed the specifics of my research process. In the rest of the book I will focus on the story of Hmong American students at University Heights High School. In chapter 2 I examine the culture of University Heights High School, my primary research site. I will describe the dominant culture of the school with an eye to how Hmong students fit into the school. In particular, I focus on the way Hmong American students were received by the larger University Heights community. I argue that the culture of UHS reflects and privileges whiteness. The questions to be addressed include: How do teachers understand and interpret Hmong American students' experiences and identities? How does the culture of whiteness shape Hmong American students' experiences at UHS?

Chapter 3 explores identity formation among Hmong American high school students. Hmong students at UHS divided themselves into two groups: "traditional" Hmong and "Americanized" Hmong. Although the students speak about the two groups as if they were rigidly dichotomous, I will explore similarities and differences between the two groups. I will examine the way "traditional" and "Americanized" students respond to school, relate to their parents, and understand issues regarding race. I argue that poverty and racism constrain identity choices for all Hmong American youth. Furthermore, I will argue that racism—the blackening of Hmong Americans and the image of Asian Americans as perpetual foreigners—informs the way Hmong American identities are understood by members of the dominant group. Finally, I will highlight examples of the hybrid nature of Hmong American youth culture and identities.

Chapter 4 focuses on the way gender, as it intersects with race, informs the immigrant experience. I will consider the various messages surrounding gender that Hmong American students receive from their families, the school, and the larger society. I consider the following questions: What does it mean to become a Hmong American man in the United States? What does it mean to become a Hmong American woman in the United States? How does gender affect the way Hmong American youth respond to life in the United States, and to schools in particular?

Chapter 5 reviews the major findings of my study with an eye to how schools can better serve the needs and interests of immigrants of color. In particular, I revisit the question regarding the characteristics of a "good" school.

By examining the experiences of one of the newer Asian American immigrant/refugee groups—Hmong Americans—this book enters the conversation about the nature of the immigrant experience today. Through a focus on Hmong American high school students, this book contributes to a growing and important conversation about the educational experiences of immigrants of color. By focusing on a group of working-class immigrants of color, this book highlights the ways that race and class influence the process of "Americanization."

2

At University Heights High School: Creating Insiders and "Others"

In terms of the traditions, in terms of the way it views itself it's really kind of a prep school. It is invested in the academic standards . . . And so it is kind of a secondary image, a secondary school, trying to be like the university, which it is very close to . . . I think if you are looking for a sort of prep school attitude toward academics . . . that is what would capture University Heights High—a public prep school.

Mr. Schenk, school social worker

Like other children of immigrants, the Hmong American youth in my study enter a very specific school culture that shapes their school experiences and their understandings of America. As one sociologist of education has said, "Immigrants do not enter undifferentiated 'American' schools. Rather they enter specific schools whose immediate contexts, histories, memories, and commitments shape their organization and practices" (Olneck, 2004, p. 386). The Hmong American students in my study attend a school known for its academic excellence. When they enter UHS, they enter a public school with a history and continuing commitment to serving the children of the educated elite of the city. Known throughout Wisconsin for its high academic standards, many consider UHS to be the best high school in the state.

While UHS has a distinct character and history of its own, it is not isolated from larger social forces. It is not exempt from the larger national conversations surrounding race. Rather, UHS is a school where national ideas regarding race intersect with local politics. As in the dominant society, whiteness defines what is normal, desirable, and good at the school. Of course, there is no single expression of whiteness or White culture in the United States, but multiple cultures of whiteness that vary depending on the ethnicity, religion, region, and social class of the community. Scholars who have focused on social class, for example, have found marked differences between the culture of middle-class Whites and working-class Whites

(Eckert, 1989; Lareau, 2000). Although there are diverse White cultures, all Whites do share White racial privilege. This chapter explores White privilege and the specific expressions of whiteness and White culture at UHS. In particular, the chapter focuses on the way the culture of whiteness at UHS shapes teachers' assumptions about the characteristics of a "good" student. I will argue that the school's culture privileges White, middle-class students, and marks Hmong American students as racialized outsiders.

Within the city of Lakeview, opinions about UHS are largely divided along race and class lines. Most White, middle-class residents praise UHS for its academic excellence and for its socially tolerant atmosphere. In contrast to this positive view of UHS, many Lakeview residents of color assert that UHS is an elitist and racist institution that has not done enough to accommodate the specific needs of the racially and economically diverse students who have entered UHS since the mid-1980s. They point to the achievement gap between students of color and White students as evidence of the problems at UHS. Like other Lakeview high schools, UHS has a particularly bad reputation for the way it serves African American students, who as a group have a districtwide average of *D*. One local newspaper with a politically progressive reputation published a piece in the mid-1990s lambasting the school for social and academic segregation along racial lines. In this particular article, Hmong students were identified as the most marginalized group at the school.

The two perspectives on UHS reflect two different definitions of racism. Many White middle-class residents of Lakeview seem to interpret the presence of a racially diverse student population and the absence of overt conflict to mean that racism does not exist at UHS. Like many White Americans, it appears that White Lakeview residents define racism as overt verbal hostility or acts of physical brutality committed by uneducated extremists. It is not insignificant that this definition of racism masks White privilege. By identifying racism as the act of extremists, middle-class White residents are able to distance themselves from racism. This perspective on race is not unique to middle-class Whites in Lakeview. Regarding the dominant perspective on race in the United States, Wu (2002) writes, "As a nation we have become so seemingly triumphant at vilifying racists that we have induced denial about racism" (p. 13). In fact, a desire to deny the significance of race has been identified as a characteristic of some White cultures (Frankenberg, 1993). For residents of color and other critics of UHS, racism includes not only overt acts of hostility, but institutional racism as well. The reality of underachievement among students of color is understood to be evidence that racial equality does not exist. In short, critics of UHS suggest, "racism must be best identified by its consequences" (Winant, 2001, p. 308).

INSIDE THE HALLS OF UHS

Hanging over the south entrance of the school is a large banner that proudly announces that UHS is a "National School of Excellence." The school's official Web site highlights its advanced academic programs and the stellar achievements of its students. The mean SAT and ACT scores for UHS students are higher than national mean scores (e.g., mean SAT scores for UHS students in 2000 were 627/verbal and 645/math compared to national mean scores of 505/verbal and 514/math). Of the 535 students in the class of 2000 who responded to the postgraduation survey, 76% reported that they planned to attend a four-year college. Of those students planning to attend a four-year college or university, 36% planned to attend a private college or university. The Web site also boasts that over 56% of the teaching staff have at least a master's degree.

Inside the school the halls are filled with trophy cases displaying the academic and athletic awards won by past and present students. On any given day a visitor to UHS might hear the principal making announcements about the students' stellar achievements (e.g., academic, athletic, artistic, service). Math and science teachers post the names of the winners of math and science competitions on their classroom doors. Grade-level principals post the names of honor roll students on their office doors. Competition and individual achievement are clearly central to the culture of the school.

In early conversations with teachers I was told repeatedly that UHS had many "talented students." One White teacher proudly stated, "My students are smarter than I am." In her description of UHS's academic mission, Mrs. Schultz, the head principal since 1992, explained, "UHS stresses getting kids to think—education for the purpose of getting kids to learn—less of an emphasis on education for work and money." Significantly, Mrs. Schultz's words echo the academic missions of many elite liberal arts colleges and private secondary schools.

In addition to the glowing descriptions of the school's many talented students and high academic standards, administrators highlighted the diversity of the student population. Mrs. Schultz, a White woman who identifies herself as an advocate of diversity, beamed as she explained that UHS was "an incredible high school—the diversity is incredible. . . . There are children of Nobel Prize winners and homeless kids, too." Mr. Smithson, the ninth-grade principal, commented on both the diverse student population and the tradition of academic excellence in his description of UHS:

> I indicate to people that this is an extremely diverse school. We
> have students here at any given time from over fifty countries
> throughout the world. We have probably the most diverse student

population in terms of ethnicity and national origin and most any other parameter you can think of, of any school I know of, certainly of any other school in the city. It is also a school with an extremely strong academic tradition, although we have programs that provide training and the possibility of careers in many areas, including business, tech ed, and so forth. In other words we are a comprehensive high school; however, our main emphasis has always been academic postsecondary preparation, and that is primarily because that is what our community has demanded of us. That is the expectation of the community.

In her introductory statement in the student handbook, Mrs. Schultz describes UHS as a "diverse community committed to excellence." Significantly, the official descriptions of UHS appear to celebrate both diversity and academic excellence.

Despite official celebrations of both academic excellence and diversity, there are signs that the school's investment in its image as an educationally elite institution overshadows its commitment to diversity. The very fact that these two commitments are seen as being distinct is itself a racist conceptualization. Although the student population at UHS has changed over the years, many UHS educators like Mr. Smithson continue to view UHS as serving a single homogeneous population. The school organization, racial composition of the staff, and school culture reflect and favor students from White middle-class students from highly educated families. It is this highly educated community that Mr. Smithson referred to as "our community" in his description of UHS.

The Role of Faculty and Staff in Reproduction of Culture

The faculty, which is almost entirely White, plays a significant role in the reproduction of the culture of UHS. UHS teachers enjoy the status associated with teaching at a school with a stellar reputation. Teachers have an average of 20 years' teaching experience, and many have been at UHS for a decade or more. Mr. Caine, a social studies teacher, explained that he loved teaching at UHS because it was like teaching at a small college. Mrs. Swanson, a relatively new member of the faculty with 6 years at UHS, explained that she felt fortunate to have landed a job at UHS as her first teaching assignment.

> *Mrs. Swanson:* I think a huge part of what makes this place such a great—and I think it is such a great place—is that the teachers mostly are very happy to be here. We have a large number of

teachers who have transferred to UHS from other places in the district as we have openings here. Because there's some prestige that comes along with teaching at UHS.

SL: Prestige within the district?

Mrs. Swanson: Within the district, within the community. UHS is an esteemed place.

SL: Can you say a bit more about that?

Mrs. Swanson: Well, we have kids who are always ranked in the highest for ACT and SAT scores. They go off to the top-notch, most prestigious universities. And the teachers get thanked for that. And I think in an age when the teachers don't necessarily get a whole lot of praise, and we've had a lot of rocky times, it's nice to be in a place where you're appreciated. And it's really nice to work in a population with kids like that, too. Our academic departments really take pride in—not just in being rigorous, but in being cutting-edge.

Most of the highest-achieving students at UHS are White or East Asian Americans from middle-class families. Thus, when Mrs. Swanson refers to "kids like that" she is implicitly referring to these students. Although most teachers speak positively about growing diversity of the student population, most teachers are unwilling and/or unsure of how to make changes to address the needs of the new populations. For them, the central purpose of UHS is to prepare "talented" (i.e., White, middle-class) students for higher education. Multicultural education is not understood to be central to this mission. In short, UHS teachers both "celebrate and ignore" diversity (Olsen, 1997).

The job of addressing the needs of diverse student populations is left largely to members of the ESL program, social workers, and a handful of specialized staff designated to serve students of color. For example, as the school's AHANA (African, Hispanic, Asian, Native American) coordinator, Mr. Buckner's primary responsibilities are to provide academic and social support for students of color. Mr. Buckner, an African American man, describes his job as being that of a "guidance counselor and social worker for students of color." Through his office he organizes college tours and runs the school's tutoring program. In addition to his full-time position as the AHANA coordinator, Mr. Buckner serves as the advisor to a few student clubs, including the Asian Club.

Ms. Bowman works part-time at UHS as the Family Community Liaison. Her primary responsibility is to serve as a liaison between families of color and the school staff, a role that gives her insight into the relationship between parents of color and UHS faculty and staff. As one of the few

African Americans on the staff, Ms. Bowman serves as a role model for students of color, and her office is a central gathering place for many African American students. In addition to her work with the African American community, Ms. Bowman served as the staff advisor for the Hmong Club during the 1998–99 academic year.

In addition to these two positions, UHS has a Home School Coordinator, Mr. Dixon, who works with students identified as having problems in school. Mr. Dixon describes his job as working with "students who are experiencing attendance, behavior, and academic problems." Although the Home School Coordinator is not identified as someone who specifically serves the community of color, Mr. Dixon explained that most of the students with whom he has had contact are non-White.

While these staff members provide crucial services, the existence of specialized staff inadvertently sends a message that issues of race and racism are somehow separate from, rather than intimately connected to, the overall culture of the school. While there are certainly individual members of the faculty and staff who make serious efforts to work with students of color, most teachers appear to see the work of addressing issues of diversity as being outside of their domain. In talking to members of the specialized staff I was struck by the fact that their work is largely isolated from the work of classroom teachers. Mrs. Bowman, for example, complained that teachers rarely seek out her advice in working with communities of color.

Defining "Talented" and "Good" Students

Teachers' definitions of "talent" reveal a bias in favor of the culture of the White educated elite. Students who score high on standardized tests like the SAT or play an instrument in the jazz band are the ones identified as "talented." On the other hand, children from immigrant families who master English as their second language are not referred to as "talented." Similarly, "good" students are defined as those who are enrolled in college preparatory classes and involved in school-sponsored sports or other extracurricular activities. Immigrant students who are enrolled in ESL classes and spend time helping with family responsibilities are not characterized in the same manner. In fact, ESL teachers complained that mainstream teachers view ESL classes as being "easy" and view ESL students who make the honor roll as being "different" than honor roll students enrolled in mainstream classes. This characterization as "easy" contributes to the stigma surrounding ESL (Olsen, 1997; Valdes, 2001).

As in other U.S. high schools, teachers at UHS defined "good" and "talented" students as those who express a proschool attitude (Eckert, 1989).

"Good" students do not challenge the school culture or structure. "Good" students are on friendly terms with faculty and staff (Eckert, 1989). They engage in witty banter with teachers and administrators inside and outside of class. In classes, "good" students express their opinions and feel free to challenge the teacher's ideas. In my observations of Mr. Caine's 12th-grade philosophy class, for example, I found students engaged in active debate similar to undergraduate seminars at elite colleges and universities. Mr. Caine called on students who apparently had reputations for playing the role of devil's advocate. Not insignificantly, the two Hmong American students in his class sat quietly while other students participated (see chapter 3 for further discussion of academic achievement). The ability to engage in witty conversation with teachers requires not only fluency in English, which all the second-generation Hmong American students have, but a specific style of speech that reflects middle-class educated norms (Bourdieu, 1984; Heath, 1983). It also requires a certain level of entitlement to assert this type of speech.

As noted earlier, "good" students participate in school-sponsored extracurricular activities. Not all school activities, however, carry equal status within the school. High-status activities were those that attracted positive publicity to the school (e.g., orchestra, jazz band, theater, varsity sports) and those that impressed college admissions officers (e.g., student government). Unlike many U.S. high schools that celebrate athletes/jocks above all other students, UHS values musicians, theater artists, and those with leadership talents as well (Foley, 1990; Lefkowitz, 1997). White middle-class students know which activities carry the highest status, and by seeking out and participating in these activities, White middle-class students confirm their own high status in the school community and confirm the status of the activities in which they participate as high. Thus, the relationship between student status and participation in high-status activities is circular and self-perpetuating.

In addition to participating in high-status extracurricular activities, UHS students must be academically strong and headed to 4-year colleges upon graduation from high school in order to be identified as "good" students. Most "good" students were either White or East Asian American. White and East Asian American students dominate the honor roll and many of the high-status extracurricular activities. While there are many nonimmigrant students of color involved in high-status sports (e.g., football and basketball), few of these students are identified as "good" students. For example, most of the awards for "student athletes" during the 2000 academic year went to White students. Low-income immigrants and second-generation students of color like Southeast Asian and Mexican students are largely absent from both the honor roll and higher-status extracurricular activities.

Although some Hmong American students are managing to do well academically, an increasing number of students are falling into academic trouble (see chapter 3). In addition to academic marginalization, most Hmong American students are socially isolated from the mainstream of the school. In my observations, for example, there were only three Hmong American students who participated in any of the higher-status extracurricular activities (e.g., athletic teams, music, theater, or student government) at UHS. Hmong American students who did participate in extracurricular activities were most likely to join either the Hmong Club or the Asian Club. It is significant, however, that both of these clubs were seen as peripheral to the school (see chapter 3).

Celebrating the Culture of Whiteness

An examination of UHS's Fine Arts Week provides another opportunity to examine the relatively privileged status of White middle-class students and the culture of whiteness at UHS. A tradition at UHS since 1972, Fine Arts Week is a celebration of performing and visual arts. Members of the UHS staff describe Fine Arts Week as a central event of the academic year. In the Fine Arts Program, Mrs. Schultz described Fine Arts Week as one of the school's "most precious treasures" that "enriches not only the student of the arts but the entire school community as well." Students in music, dance, and theater groups and classes perform at assemblies throughout the week before groups of students, teachers, and parents. Students in the visual arts display pottery, paintings, metalworks, and other artwork produced in classes.

Significantly, the majority of students who participate in Fine Arts Week are White and middle-class. Ms. Heinemann, the chair of the ESL department, explained that many of the students who perform at Fine Arts Week have had private music and dance lessons since they were young children. Few students of color participate and even fewer immigrants of color perform or display their art. The only explicitly multicultural performances during Fine Arts Week are presented by the multicultural theater group, which includes a racially and ethnically diverse group of UHS students. During the 1998–99 school year one Hmong American boy performed with this multicultural theater group.

During the 1998–99 school year, a group of students of color organized the first Diversity Days celebration in response to what they perceived to be the Eurocentric nature of Fine Arts Week. Rita, a South Asian American student who spearheaded the event, explained:

In the Fine Arts Week celebration, there's nothing that is very diverse. We want to have a Diversity Week celebration where we could show off different art like dancing and performances; where we have panels and discussion in classes about diverse issues, you know?

As a self-described student activist, Rita asserted that she wanted to "make people aware" of the cultures of nonmainstream students. She explained that some students interpreted Diversity Days as divisive: "Some mainstream students say stuff like 'Why do you need it?'" The differences between Diversity Days and Fine Arts Week were many. While the great majority of students who participated in Fine Arts week were White, most of the students who participated in Diversity Days were students of color. Although faculty and staff were certainly supportive of Diversity Days, they were much more enthusiastic about Fine Arts Week. Students who performed during Fine Arts Week were described as being "super talented," and students who performed during Diversity Days were seen as performing "interesting" or "traditional" arts. In other words, the musical and artistic talent most valued is raced and classed in White and middle-class ways. Hmong American students who practiced traditional Hmong dancing or singing were seen as engaging in exotic cultural practices. They simply were not seen as "talented" singers or dancers.

Diversity Days can be read as an act of student resistance on the part of students of color. In response to their perceived exclusion from Fine Arts Week, Rita and her peers were determined that the artistic expressions of students of color would be seen and heard by all students at the school. Diversity Days quickly developed a reputation for being the school's multicultural week. Diversity Days gave a few Hmong students an opportunity to be seen by their non-Hmong peers for one brief moment. For example, a group of girls from the Hmong Club performed Hmong dances dressed in Hmong garb. The president of the Hmong Club explained that although she was nervous about performing in front of a non-Hmong crowd, she was pleased to have the opportunity to share her culture. Although non-Hmong students were exposed to a few Hmong dances, it appeared that many non-Hmong students did not know anything about who the Hmong are or why they are in the United States. During one performance, for example, I overheard a group of White students describe the Hmong dancers as "Tibetan dancers."

Although the students who participated in Diversity Days were proud to show off their cultures, I would argue that Diversity Days had limited educational value. Like other ethnic festivals or celebrations, Diversity Days may have unintentionally perpetuated ethnic stereotypes (Nieto, 2000;

Perry, 2001). As is common with superficial forms of multicultural education, Diversity Days inadvertently contributed to the identification of students of color as being culturally different while simultaneously erasing
White culture(s) (Kenny, 2000; Perry, 2001). Finally, I would argue that
it failed to challenge larger assumptions regarding what constitutes art.

Reproducing the Racial Hierarchy

UHS educators who work most closely with students of color fear that the
culture at UHS is reproducing existing racial and economic inequalities.
Like the outside critics of UHS, these educators point to the achievement
gap as evidence that racial inequalities persist. They point out that while
there are some White teachers who are culturally sensitive, these teachers
are far and few between. Furthermore, they assert that most teachers see
the children of the educated elite as their only constituency.

Ms. Bowman, the Family Community Liaison, claimed that many teachers see any efforts to address issues of diversity as unnecessary and even
threatening to the elite culture of the school. Mr. Burns, a grade-level principal and an African American man who graduated from UHS in the early
1980s, observes that the student population has changed dramatically since
his student days. Burns believes that the low achievement levels among
many students of color reflect the fact that many teachers do not know how
to work with diverse populations. Furthermore, he suggested that most
teachers are uninterested in learning about the unique needs of students of
color, a fact that was largely confirmed by my observations. In discussing
the racial situation at UHS, Mr. Burns said, "I mean, even though . . . we
have a diverse student population, I think there's still, you know, some sort
of elemental power relative to those subsets." Here, Mr. Burns appears to
be referring to the racial hierarchy at UHS that, like the racial hierarchy in
the larger society, places Whites on top. Similarly, Mr. Schenk, a middle-
aged White man who works with many students of color in his capacity as
a school social worker, suggested that the school was a much more friendly
place for White middle-class students. Schenk described the Hmong student
community as among the most isolated and marginalized.

Mr. Schenk, Mr. Burns, Ms. Bowman, and others who work closely
with students of color assert that the school needs to diversify the teaching staff and the curriculum in order to reach students of color. Although
Mrs. Schultz agrees that more needs to be done to address the needs of
students of color, she asserts that the school culture has changed in recent
years to become more inclusive. Mrs. Schultz explained that during her
tenure as head principal she has worked to hire a more representative staff
because she believes that it is the key to higher achievement among stu-

dents of color. She also stated that she supports multicultural education and has spearheaded the multicultural retreats for selected students. The multicultural retreat gives a small group of students an opportunity to spend concentrated time discussing issues of diversity. Most students at UHS, however, were unaffected and even unaware of the retreats.

Although Mrs. Schultz's supporters credit her with supporting multicultural efforts and with the increasing presence of African American administrators at UHS, some expressed pessimism regarding any real change at the school. Mr. Schenk, for example, asserted that significant changes in the school culture are unlikely to occur.

> And you will hear all kinds of talk about, well, as the older teachers retire and the younger teachers come in we will start to see a curriculum and instructional strategies that are more reflective of the population we are dealing with. I, frankly, haven't seen that much of a shift. I don't think as an organization it has shifted. There are individuals and almost all of the individuals, including a lot of the old-timers, are really kid-oriented, but . . . There is always this kind of notion that somehow or another the school's culture is going to change. But I don't think it has changed very much and I don't know that it would.

Mr. Schenk went on to observe that the school has consistently chosen to support programs that serve elite students even at the cost of programs that target more diverse populations.

Mrs. Schultz admits that efforts to diversify the teaching staff have been limited. According to Mrs. Schultz, the hiring guidelines enforced by the teachers' union are to blame for the largely White faculty. During the 1998–99 school year, there were two Asian American bilingual resource specialists and one Asian American teacher on the staff. The teacher taught Japanese language on a part-time basis. Not insignificantly, a number of Hmong American students indicated interest in taking Japanese language because they wanted to learn about "other Asian cultures." During the 1999–2000 school year, there were three Asian American bilingual resource specialists on staff, and no certified Asian American teachers. Most of the Hmong American students at UHS had never had a teacher of color and had never met an Asian American teacher. Several students were, in fact, surprised to learn that I, an Asian American woman, was a professor at the university they dreamed of attending.

The whiteness of the UHS faculty reflects the whiteness of the Wisconsin teaching force, which is 91% White, and the teaching force across the country, which is largely White, female, monolingual, and middle-class

(Goodwin, 2002; Rong & Preissle, 1997; Snyder & Hoffman, 1994). Much of the research on White teachers' attitudes regarding student diversity suggests that teachers know little about the cultural background of students of color and/or view the problems experienced by students of color as being rooted in their own backgrounds (Goodwin, 2002; Kailin, 1999; King, 1991; Nieto, 2000). As I have argued thus far in this chapter, the whiteness of the UHS faculty and staff shapes educational opportunities for students of color. Like others, I would argue that the shortage of teachers of color means that students of color lack role models of color in school, a fact that can negatively influence their educational aspirations (Goodwin, 2002). Furthermore, the whiteness of the UHS faculty contributes to Hmong students' views that Whites are the only true Americans. The relative absence of Asian Americans on the UHS staff reinforces Hmong American students' ideas that Asian Americans are not real Americans.

An examination of the school's curriculum revealed that there were few courses devoted to multicultural issues. Despite the rhetoric regarding the importance of diversity, multicultural education is not central to the school's curriculum. One course in the English department has an explicit focus on multiculturalism (Contemporary Multicultural Literature), and two courses in the Social Studies department focus explicitly on multiculturalism (U.S. History/African American Experience and Conflict Resolution in Multicultural Education). The only required course that addresses multicultural issues is the U.S. history course that covers a wide range of issues including the Cold War, McCarthyism, the Korean and Vietnam wars, and "the struggle for social justice and equal opportunity of African Americans, Asian Americans, Hispanic Americans, Native Americans, and women" (1999–2000 Course of Study Handbook, p. 39). As noted earlier in this chapter, there were isolated examples of multicultural efforts, but these were not integrated into the core of the curriculum or the core of the school culture.

The relative absence of multicultural content in the curriculum likely reflects the commonly held perspective among educators that multicultural education is only for students of color (Nieto, 2000). Since many White UHS educators appear to view the children of the White, educated elite to be their primary constituency, they also assume that multicultural education is unnecessary. This perspective fails to acknowledge the fact that multicultural education is important for all students because it more accurately reflects the reality of the United States and the larger world (Banks, 1995; Bennett, 1999; Lewis, 2001; Nieto, 2000; Sleeter & Grant, 1999).

As other scholars have previously argued, decisions about curriculum are always political, never neutral (Apple, 1993, 1996; Nieto, 2000). The curriculum represents the official knowledge of the school and reflects the interests of those in power. As Apple (1996) argues, "What *counts* as knowledge, the ways in which it is organized, who is empowered to teach it, what counts as an appropriate display of having learned it, and—just as critically—who is allowed to ask and answer all these questions, are part and parcel of how dominance and subordination are reproduced and altered in this society" (p. 22). Furthermore, students pick up social messages from what is included and what is excluded from the curriculum (Apple, 1993, 1996; Nieto, 2000). Nieto (2000) states, "The curriculum lets students know whether the knowledge they and their communities value has prestige within the educational establishment" (p. 96). At UHS the largely Eurocentric curriculum tells Hmong American students that they are not important, and it also tells them that whiteness is central to being American.

Privileging "Good" Parents

The social, cultural, and class positions reflected in definitions of "good" students are also reflected in the implicit definitions of "good" parents. Many UHS educators have implicit definitions of "good" parents, who express their concern for their children's education by becoming involved in the day-to-day activities of the school. UHS encourages various types of parental involvement from volunteering and communication with the school to decision-making (Epstein, 1992, 1995).

Parents can volunteer to support various student activities (e.g., athletics, drama, chorus, band, orchestra). During Fine Arts Week, for example, a hospitality room is set up at the school for parents who attend student performances. In terms of decision-making, parents have opportunities to participate on the grade-level advisory boards and to be involved in the Parent Teacher Student Organization (PTSO). The PTSO publishes a monthly newsletter that serves as an avenue for school-to-home communication (Epstein, 1992, 1995). A parent group meets monthly to help parents/guardians network and support each other in issues related to parenting teens.

As in many schools, White parents from higher social class and educational backgrounds are the most involved in the school, particularly the decision-making types of activities (Comer, 1980; Fine, 1993). Middle-class/educated parents have the flexible schedules that allow them to be highly involved in their children's education (Doerfler, 2001). It is not uncommon to see White parents attending student assemblies during school hours. Their knowledge of and comfort with the school culture allow them to participate in their children's education in ways that are accepted by school officials (Comer, 1980; Doerfler, 2001; Lareau, 2000). During the 1998–99 school year, for example, the co-president of the PTSO was a university professor. Finally, highly educated parents can serve as informal teachers by assisting their children with homework. Similar to educators at other schools, most UHS educators view the involvement of middle-class/educated parents as "normal" interest in their children's education (Lareau, 1989; Valdes, 1996). Furthermore, they assume that parental involvement is central to high student achievement. Mr. Smithson asserted that students who are "tracking and doing well" have parents who are interested and involved in their education.

Like other UHS educators, Mr. Smithson defined parental involvement in White middle-class terms. Many teachers assumed that parents who did not make their presence felt in the school were not involved in the children's education. On numerous occasions, for example, I heard UHS staff lament that they could not get parents of color to participate on the PTSO. Like other low-income parents of color, most Hmong parents do not have the time, resources, and/or knowledge to influence the school policy or engage in the day-to-day activities of the school (Doerfler, 2001; Lareau, 2000; Valdes, 1996).

Hmong immigrant parents, like other low-income immigrants, rarely initiate contact with the school; instead they come into the school only when a teacher or administrator directly requests their presence (Valdes, 1996). Hmong American students reported that their parents felt uncomfortable coming to the school because of their limited English skills and their limited understanding of the school system. During my fieldwork I did observe and/or hear of parents who came to UHS to meet with administrators. Unfortunately, in these cases Hmong parents had been called to the school because their children were having academic difficulties or problems with truancy. Mrs. Her, one of the Hmong bilingual resource specialists at UHS, explained that this pattern served to reinforce the barrier between families and schools. In an effort to address the truancy problem among Hmong American students, UHS administrators asked Hmong parents to follow their children during school for a day. While this practice may have served to inform parents about life in their child's school, it also served to further marginalize Hmong American students.

Although many UHS staff assumed that Hmong parents were not involved in their children's education, through conversations with Hmong American students, I learned that many Hmong parents were actively involved in the education of their children. Their manner of involvement, however, was either unseen or unappreciated by UHS staff. All students reported that their parents counseled them to work hard in school. Like many immigrant parents, Hmong parents believe that education is important for economic success. One student explained, "Hmong parents tell you to go to school. Don't skip. Do your homework when you come home. Go to the library, if possible. Get a book and check it out and read."

Each year the United Refugee Services sponsors a graduation ceremony to honor Southeast Asian American high school seniors from throughout the Lakeview School District. The most active Hmong parents participated in this annual event. When I attended the Southeast Asian Graduation in May 2000 I saw several Hmong students there with their parents and siblings. Speaking in Hmong and then in English, a Hmong man from United Refugee Services congratulated the seniors and encouraged them to make good decisions in their lives.

Hmong American students reported that problems in school were among the most common sources of intergenerational conflict. One young woman related that her parents took her to see a shaman in an effort to get her to stop skipping school. Another student reported that his parents had requested that his sister be allowed to attend another high school because they were afraid that she had gotten involved with "bad" Hmong kids. These examples all clearly demonstrate that Hmong parents are involved in their children's educations and view truancy to be a major problem.

Pang, a senior in the class of 1999, explained that his father and mother have always encouraged him to do well in school, but can't help him with his academic work because they have little formal education. Reflecting on his father's involvement in his education, Pang said, "When my sisters and I were little, our dad gave us paper and pen and said, 'This is what you need for school.'" Although Pang appreciates his parents' support, he was quick to point out that his parents are unable to help him in the ways that "American" parents can. Pang feels that he is at a disadvantage when competing with his "American" (read White middle-class) peers because they can turn to their parents for help with schoolwork. When Pang learned that my mother was a high school math teacher, he said, "You are really lucky, you know." In fact, Pang is at a disadvantage because UHS values and expects the type of parental involvement exhibited by White middle-class parents. Pang's parents, like other Hmong American parents, lack the cultural and social capital to help their children with academic work and/or to effectively advocate for them in the school.

Hmong immigrant parents also appeared to have culturally different ideas about the role of teachers and schools in their children's lives. Mr. Burns relayed that Hmong parents often expressed dismay at the school's inability to force children to go to school. While the school assumes that it is the parent's responsibility to address truancy issues, Hmong immigrant parents assume that the schools should be able to do something to make the children attend school. In her work as a Hmong bilingual resource specialist, Mrs. Her has had many opportunities to observe exchanges between parents and UHS staff. With regard to truancy, Mrs. Her stated, "The school blames the parents and the parents blame the school." Hmong immigrant parents assume that schools will exercise disciplinary authority over their children as those in Laos, and they are frustrated when schools can't control their children. Like other immigrant parents, Hmong parents assume that schools take responsibility for the academic and moral education of their children (Valdes, 1996). Hmong parents, for example, expect schools to teach children to be good and to respect their elders.

Educators who express concern for students of color suggest that the inequality among students is related to the inequality among UHS parents. These educators point to the power of elite parents to control and reproduce the elite school culture. Mr. Burns, for example, maintained that the UHS is most responsive to students from highly educated families because their parents pressure the school to serve their interests. UHS educators explained that the highly educated parents exert a great deal of influence over the school because they understand and know how to manipulate the unwritten rules that govern schools. These parents know which courses and activities will impress college admissions officers, and they make every effort to ensure that their children have advantages. They know about various scholarships and awards and they are invested in helping their children win them. In short, the highly educated parents possess the entitlement and the type of cultural capital recognized by UHS and by institutions of higher education (Bourdieu, 1984; Doerfler, 2001; Lareau, 1989). Other researchers have identified a similar pattern of responding to the demand of powerful parents (Gitlin et al., 2003; Metz, 1986). Gitlin et al. found, "A concern for white parents quickly becomes a concern for the school because those parents had the economic and social power to make strong demands on teachers and administrator" (p. 115).

According to Mr. Schenk, the needs of lower-income students are often overlooked because their parents "don't do much and can't because they don't have the resources." Similarly, Mr. Burns lamented that "Black kids and Hmong kids don't have parents who come in here making all kinds of demands." In her position as the Family Community Liaison, Ms. Bowman works to empower the participation of communities of color. Although she has had some success working with the African American community, cultural and language differences have thus far limited her efforts with the Southeast Asian communities. In short, Hmong American students and other low-income students of color do not have parents who possess the cultural capital recognized by UHS, and who therefore cannot influence the school to meet their children's needs (Bourdieu, 1984; Lareau, 1989).

Many White UHS educators consistently referred to the educational and class backgrounds of the parents and students who were highly involved in the school, but they were virtually silent about the fact that most of these students and parents are White. Interestingly, many of these educators did mention that "students of color" or "minority" students were struggling at the school. Significantly, students of color were the only ones marked racially. In their explanations of the advantages that elite students and parents possessed, White educators (even UHS staff like Mr. Schenk who expressed concern about students of color) emphasized the significance of class over race. Thus, class and educational background are codes for whiteness at UHS. In discussing the relationship between middle class status and constructions of ideal whiteness, Kenny (2000) writes:

> Whiteness is also, among other things, a classed position, tempered through and recognizable as "cultural capital" (Bourdieu 1984): the ability to have access to and make optimum use of things like higher education and the learned social graces, vocabularies and demeanors that allow one to prosper among the elite or at least compete within the dominant culture. (p. 7)

Here, Kenny is referencing a White, middle-class, educated culture. It is this expression of whiteness that dominates the UHS culture. By emphasizing the significance of class over race, the White educators sidestepped the issue of White privilege. They were engaging in the race and power evasiveness associated with White talk (Frankenberg, 1993). My argument is not that they were intentionally evading their privilege, but rather that the denial of White privilege may simply reflect a lack of awareness regarding whiteness common among White middle-class individuals (McIntosh, 1989; Weiler, 1988).

At UHS, White middle-class cultural norms set the standards by which students were made either insiders or outsiders. The culture of whiteness set the tone for what was considered to be "normal" in terms of achievement and future aspirations. Importantly, whiteness remained largely invisible. About the invisibility of whiteness, Fiske writes, "This refusal of definition is crucial to the process of othering that has long been recognized as a key white strategy of colonialization" (p. 42). This virtual invisibility and silence served to normalize whiteness and thereby maintain its dominance at UHS (Dyer, 1993; Fiske, 1994; Frankenberg, 1993; Rains, 1998; Weiler, 1988). Rains explains:

> This belief of "white is the norm" is so ingrained it remains obscured from view, as natural as the air we breathe but do not see. This inability to see something that truly affects all of our lives contributes to the invisibility of white privilege as a corollary to racism. (p. 80)

More recent scholarship on whiteness has challenged the idea that whiteness is invisible, asking for whom whiteness is invisible and under what circumstances. Frankenberg (2001) has recently argued that Whites, particularly those who may feel that people of color threaten their positions, are reasserting whiteness. I would argue that the invisibility of whiteness at UHS is due to the secure status of whiteness at the school.

The culture of whiteness at UHS privileged White middle-class students from highly educated families and disadvantaged Hmong American students and other low-income students of color. In short, the "prep school" culture (i.e., culture of whiteness) at UHS effectively excludes Hmong students and other low-income students of color. Within this culture of whiteness at UHS, cultural differences were given lip service, but they were not truly valued and they did not change the mainstream culture of the school. It is important to point out that overt forms of racial hostility were not a part of the UHS culture. Instead, the school was permeated with what Gallagher (2000) refers to as a "filtered and perfumed racism" that is hidden "by use of qualifiers, caveats and appeals to meritocratic and individualistic principles" (p. 67). The fact that the culture of whiteness is hidden behind meritocratic and color-blind rhetoric makes it particularly difficult to challenge.

While I was working on revisions of this chapter in the fall of 2003, a racial controversy erupted in the Lakeview School District that reflects the dominance of the culture of whiteness and the concomitant denial of racism throughout the Lakeview District and the city. In an effort to address the achievement gap between students of color and White students, the superintendent invited an antiracist scholar and educator to present a series of workshops for Lakeview educators during the 2003–04 academic year. The reactions to the first required workshop ranged from supportive to defensive. While some teachers, parents, and Lakeview residents wrote editorials in local newspapers in which they praised the workshops as a step toward addressing racial inequality, others questioned the value of the workshop and even the qualifications of the workshop facilitator, who was a Stanford-educated African American man.

An unsigned e-mail sent over the Lakeview School District Listserv criticized the workshop. The writer, who self-identified as a teacher, suggested that the blame for student underachievement rested with families of color. As evidence that all is well with the Lakeview schools, the writer pointed out that the schools are considered to be among the best in the country and "Our students excel nationally in the SAT/ACT scores." The writer continued, "Everyone knows that the single greatest determinant for childhood success relies on parental intervention strategies, not race workshops for teachers." Throughout the letter the writer relied on commonly accepted ideas regarding parent involvement to blame families of color for their children's underachievement in school. Like many of the UHS faculty in my study, the writer of the letter appears to hold unquestioned assumptions regarding proper parental involvement and the abilities of all families to be involved in schools. The writer called upon the rhetoric of color blindness to argue against what he/she perceived to be an overemphasis on the role of race and racism on student achievement. The writer stated, "Many whites don't think about color simply because we are not obsessed with it. Conversely, minorities will predictably react as the victim to ensure pity which translates into leniency and/or government activism."

While the letter can be interpreted as an isolated act of an extreme individual, I would argue that this type of color-blind rhetoric and denial of racism underlie the culture of whiteness at UHS and the larger society. Like many UHS educators, the writer of this letter assumed that the high achievement of many White middle-class students confirmed that the schools were doing their jobs. The assumption is that students of color who fail are doing so because of their families' shortcomings and their own lack of effort, not because the schools fail them. It is exactly this meritocratic rhetoric that supports the status quo.

In the last section of this chapter I will focus on how the culture of whiteness influenced the way UHS educators interpreted the academic and social experiences of their Hmong American students.

A MATTER OF "CULTURE": INTERPRETATIONS OF HMONG AMERICAN STUDENTS' EXPERIENCES

In discussing the academic problems and/or social isolation that many Hmong American students experienced, most educators at UHS relied on explanations that centered on culture. The first version of the cultural explanation advanced by many UHS educators focused on the *cultural differences* between Hmong culture and mainstream American culture. UHS educators who reflected this perspective echoed many of the assumptions advocated by cultural difference/discontinuity theorists (e.g., Au & Mason, 1981; Erickson & Mohatt, 1982; Heath, 1983; Philips, 1982). According to cultural difference/discontinuity scholars, the problems that many children of color face in school are due to cultural differences/mismatches between the students' home culture and the school culture. Significantly, cultural difference theorists do not negatively judge the home cultures of nonmainstream children, but instead argue that while their cultures are inherently valuable, they do not match the mainstream culture represented

in schools. Furthermore, they suggest that schools need to adopt culturally sensitive pedagogy to accommodate the cultural differences of the
students.

Like the cultural difference scholars, many UHS educators suggested
that *cultural differences* created difficulties for Hmong American students.
Many White teachers, for example, asserted that the issues that Hmong
American students faced were related to language. Implicit in their assumption was the idea that the Hmong language is a "problem" rather than a
"resource" (Ruiz, 1984). Although UHS educators who advanced this explanation did not explicitly judge the Hmong culture, many used the cultural explanation to free themselves of any responsibility for serving
Hmong American students. Some teachers, for example, simply assumed
that once Hmong American students became more "Americanized" (i.e.,
like White middle-class students) and became English-language-fluent that
they would be integrated into the mainstream of UHS culture. Here, the
assumptions seemed to be that Hmong American students will inevitably
assimilate into the dominant culture and that once they do they will no
longer have problems.

Their assumptions regarding the inevitability of assimilation are based
on classical assimilation theories that describe a rather linear path from
immigrant to mainstream American. Several White educators at UHS, for
example, mentioned being the grandchildren or great-grandchildren of
European immigrants. In particular, they referred to the loss of language
and other cultural traits that occurred in their families over the course of
a few generations. For these educators, cultural identity was a distant
memory or something that they called upon during holiday celebrations.
Ethnicity had become something that was optional (Waters, 1990). Although not explicitly stated, their stories served as examples that assimilation is necessary and inevitable. Their stories also served to reinforce the
dominant idea that immigrant struggle results ultimately in triumph.

Although well-intentioned, these teachers fail to recognize that their
vision of assimilation fails to consider that experiences of immigrants of
color are qualitatively different from experiences of European immigrants
(Omi & Winant, 1986; Sleeter, 1993; Waters, 1990). The dominant image
of assimilation is based on the assumptions of color blindness. It fails to
consider the way racism structures and limits the life opportunities of
people of color. Furthermore, it fails to recognize the existence of the White
privilege that allows White ethnics to choose whether or not to identify
with their ethnic group. Arguing that ethnicity is imposed on ethnics of
color, Waters (1990) writes, "For the ways in which ethnicity is flexible
and symbolic and voluntary for white middle class Americans are the very
ways in which it is not so for non-white and Hispanic Americans . . . The

social and political consequences of being Asian or Hispanic or black are not symbolic for the most part, or voluntary" (p. 156).

Many of the UHS educators who advanced a *cultural difference* explanation believed that the ESL department should handle any educational issues that involved culture. Their implicit assumption seemed to be that the ESL department was best equipped to work with culturally different students. Ms. Heinemann, chair of the ESL department in the 1998–99 year, complained that most non-ESL teachers at UHS have abdicated responsibility for students they view as culturally different. According to Ms. Heinemann, many teachers refer Hmong students, even those who are not enrolled in the ESL department, to ESL as soon as they experience academic difficulties. She argued that:

> the school needs to recognize the population of students who are born and educated here and still don't feel part of the mainstream curriculum, the mainstream school activities . . . I don't think those students should be counted as ESL students, because that makes them more different, that separates them more.

The practice of referring all Hmong students to ESL reflects the fact that most mainstream teachers lack both the interest and knowledge to work with second-language students. Similarly, in her study on Latino students, Valdes (2001) discovered that most mainstream teachers preferred not to have nonnative speakers in their classes. Mainstream teachers at UHS seemed to assume that nonmainstream students were the only students affected by culture and that cultural issues fall outside the purview of the regular educational program. This reflects the assumption that mainstream American culture is somehow normal and natural. The segregation of culturally different students ensures that the mainstream culture of the school remains untouched and unchanged.

Ms. Heinemann suggests that the school's practice of sending students to ESL for help has contributed to the stigmatization of ESL students. Mr. Henry, an older White man who has worked as a guidance counselor in the district for decades, admits that there is a stigma associated with being in ESL, but he suggests that the stigma is only in the minds of ESL students: "There's some stigma. You need this special treatment, you're not smart like I am. But I think it's mostly, though, in the ESL kids' heads." While Ms. Heinemann appreciates the role of the school in stigmatizing ESL students, Mr. Henry simply blames the victim. This victim-blaming perspective is common at UHS and ultimately serves to leave UHS practices unquestioned.

Once again, the culture of whiteness at UHS remained invisible. Culture was understood to be embodied in the Other. Operating as the unmarked norm, whiteness marks the "other" as different (Frankenberg, 1993; McLaren, 1998). As in the dominant society, whiteness is implicitly associated with American-ness. Frankenberg notes that White culture "is inflected by nationhood, such that whiteness and Americanness, though by no means coterminous, are profoundly shaped by one another . . ." (1993, p. 233). Similarly, Hurtado and Stewart (1997) have argued "In the United States, national identity has been construed as white. To be non white is to be non-American" (p. 305).

As non-Whites, Hmong Americans are viewed as culturally different (i.e., foreign) and therefore un-American. As culturally different "foreigners," Hmong American students are understood to be outside the responsibility of the regular educators. Although it might appear that Hmong American students at UHS are viewed as "foreigners" simply because they are relative newcomers to the United States, it is important to recall that Asian Americans have historically been cast as perpetual foreigners in the United States (Lei, 2001; Lowe, 1996; Tuan, 1998). Lowe (1996) argues that Asian Americans represent the "foreigner within" in the U.S. imagination. At UHS, "foreigners" were understood to be the responsibility of the ESL department.

While many UHS educators characterized Hmong American students as *culturally different* (i.e., foreign), a few members of the UHS staff characterized Hmong students as *culturally deficient*. These educators reflected the position of the cultural deficiency literature of the 1960s and the "at-risk" literature of the 1980s and 1990s (Hess & Shipman, 1965). Unlike cultural difference/discontinuity theorists, who support a culturally relativistic perspective, scholars who focus on cultural deficiency/deprivation argue that nonmainstream children are disadvantaged/deprived by their home cultures (e.g., Hess & Shipman, 1965; Lewis, 1966). According to this perspective, poor and minority cultures are inherently inferior to mainstream White middle-class culture. Some researchers who support this explanation argue that poor children are trapped in a "culture of poverty" that prevents them from taking advantage of educational opportunities (Lewis, 1966).

In contrast to their colleagues who emphasized *cultural differences*, the UHS educators who advanced the *cultural deficit* discourse made more explicitly negative judgments about Hmong students' culture. Their descriptions of Hmong culture reflected much of the scholarly and popular literature on Hmong immigrants that has cast Hmong culture as preliterate, traditional, clannish, rural, and patriarchal. According to this literature, the economic and social problems faced by the Hmong American community are almost exclusively rooted in their culture. The practice of early marriage and early childbearing for girls has been identified as the major barrier to girls' educations (Goldstein, 1985; Rumbaut & Ima, 1988;

Walker-Moffat, 1995). Similarly, many UHS educators identified early marriage as the primary reason that Hmong American girls could not take advantage of the educational opportunities at UHS. These educators constructed the practice of early marriage as "backwards." Mrs. Smith, a guidance counselor, suggested that Hmong girls who followed the path of early marriage were doomed to economic failure beyond the control of the schools. A White woman in her mid-forties, Mrs. Smith suggested that education should introduce students to a new and better way of life. When she spoke about Hmong American girls who had chosen to marry early, she appeared visibly disgusted. Although early marriage does in fact create obstacles for some Hmong American female students, the suggestion that early marriage is the proximate cause of the educational troubles faced by some Hmong American girls fails to consider the role that schools play in their school experiences. The construction of early marriage as "backwards" fails to recognize the particular social, economic, and historical contexts in which early marriage was practiced in Laos (Lynch, 1999). Furthermore, this explanation fails to recognize that the Hmong American community holds complex and diverse attitudes toward the practice of early marriage (Lee, 2001a).

Other UHS educators assumed that most Hmong American students had not learned the value of education at home. Mr. Henry suggested that Southeast Asian students are intellectually lazy.

> *Mr. Henry:* A lot of them are not intellectually motivated. These are Southeast Asians I'm talking about now. They are polite, they're nice, they never tell me what, where to go and that sort of thing, I'm a counselor. But they don't have a background of working hard academically, and they don't feel like it now.
>
> *SL:* So, you've found that it is a struggle for you to motivate them?
>
> *Mr. Henry:* They don't seem to buy into this, I guess this foolish idea that we have of working hard, keeping your nose to the grindstone.

Mr. Henry assumed that the academic problems that Southeast Asian students experienced were due to a lack of motivation. Similarly, Mr. Dixon, a member of the support staff, maintained that some students of color, including Hmong students, come from families that don't value education:

> African American kids, Hmong kids, Hispanic kids . . . Some families, you know I shouldn't generalize, but some families are . . . some push those kids to go and get education and are very

pro-education. Some families have a kind of culture of not being
involved in schools and not valuing education. So it's kind of
sometimes put on a back burner . . . the immediate needs of the
family come first. Some kids might have to get a job, they might
have to baby-sit sometimes when they are the only option, so they
might miss school.

Because Mr. Dixon did not observe the type of parental involvement pre-
scribed by White middle-class standards, he assumed that many minority
families simply did not have the right priorities. Similar to teachers at other
multiracial schools, Mr. Dixon and many other UHS educators assumed
that low-income parents devalue education (Lipman, 1998).

Some UHS educators who advanced the *cultural deficit* perspective
believed that many Hmong students were falling into negative patterns
as a result of living in poverty. Here, the problem was seen as being related to social class and not the Hmong culture. These educators asserted
that some Hmong students had become Americanized in a "bad way" and
were "at risk" for becoming the "new underclass." Mr. Dixon explained
that a growing number of Hmong parents had lost control over their children and that students from these families were "at risk" of falling into a
pattern of chronic truancy and problems with the law. Several teachers
and administrators expressed fears about what they perceived to be the
growing gang problem in the Hmong community. Although there was not
any evidence of widespread gang involvement among Hmong American
students at UHS, the baggy pants and baseball caps worn by many of the
youth were seen as evidence of possible gang affiliation. Additionally, the
fact that many Hmong American students spoke English in a dialect associated with urban youth of color led some educators to conclude that
Hmong American youth were being pulled into the "bad aspects of American culture."

Significantly, the clothing and language styles that many Hmong American youth adopted were associated with urban youth of color, specifically
African American youth. Within the mainstream media, music styles and
clothing styles associated with African American youth are characterized as
rejecting good and legitimate dominant American values. Rap music, for
example, is represented as violent, resistant, racist, sexist, and dangerous
(Kelley, 1997; Koza, 1994). Thus, "bad" Americanization seemed to be code
for things associated with blackness. On the other hand, "good" American
ways were implicitly associated with White middle-class culture.

UHS educators who advanced the *cultural deficit* (i.e., "at risk") perspective seemed to believe that the students' problems lay outside the
school. According to these educators, many Hmong students simply lack

the appropriate support for education within the home. Mr. Dixon, for example, asserted that it was nearly impossible for schools to help students from "dysfunctional families."

> *SL:* Is there anything schools can do in that situation?
> *Mr. Dixon:* I thought about that. I thought about that . . . the idealistic answer is that schools should reach out to some of these families and kids. But how do you, you know, actually reach? You know, effectively do that? Is it the job of the school to do that? At some level, you have to hold the students accountable and to hold the family accountable . . . I know that there are families that want to do the right thing, but do not know how to do that. I think that support staff can help them do that. But I think that it has to be initiated by the families.

As a self-identified mixed-race individual, Mr. Dixon seemed to identify with students of color. He struggled with how to help "at-risk" Hmong American, African American, and Latino students, but because he saw the problem as coming from the families, he concluded that the school could only wait for the families to initiate change. Similarly, in identifying early marriage as the central barrier to education for Hmong girls, Mrs. Smith and others have located the problem within the Hmong culture and therefore outside the school. Although early marriage does present impediments for some Hmong American girls, educators who focused on cultural deficiencies rarely considered what the schools might do to better serve girls who marry early at their parents' insistence or by choice (Lee, 2001a).

Some non-Hmong students have also begun to characterize Hmong American students as culturally deficient. Unlike UHS educators, who often used terms like "underclass" and "at risk," students were more likely to use an overtly racialized discourse. Rita, the South Asian American student described earlier in this chapter, explained that many non-Asians stereotype Hmong students in overtly negative ways.

> Like the stereotypes that people have are like a lot of the Hmong— the Hmong stereotype is that they're all gangsters and they follow, like, the "black path" of wearing baggy clothes and being cool and forming gangs and not coming to school, and being truant, you know, all the time.

In conversations with other non-Hmong students I was struck by the fact that Hmong American students were consistently described as having a "ghetto style" or "gang style." UHS educators and students who describe Hmong Americans in terms of cultural deficiency are engaging in an ideological blackening of Hmong American students (Ong, 1999). While Hmong American and other Southeast Asian students were ideologically blackened, East Asian American students experienced a different reading. Mr. Henry, for example, explained that East Asian students were "more serious" than Southeast Asian students. He explained: "Other kids that are Asian-looking and have probably . . . maybe have Asian parents and that sort of thing . . . are number three in the class, who have been accepted at Yale and that sort of thing."

Similarly, Mr. Smithson informed me that many East Asian students were "outstripping White kids in terms of attendance and probably achievement as well." Significantly, Asian American students who did well academically and participated in extracurricular activities were described as "Americanized" (i.e., like the White middle class) and therefore ideologically whitened. As in other schools, the "model minority" success of some Chinese American and Korean American students was used by some UHS educators as evidence that equal opportunity existed at UHS (Lee, 1996). It is important to point out, however, that these successful Asian Americans were described as "Americanized" and not as "American." Thus, while they were ideologically whitened, they were not granted full status as Americans.

At UHS, both the discourse of *cultural difference* and that of *cultural deficiency* reflect the assumptions of cultural racism (Balibar, 1992; Winant, 2001). While an emphasis on *cultural difference* was supposedly based on nonjudgmental and non-hierarchical assessments of Hmong culture, it was still exclusive in nature. It served to highlight an "us" and "them" way of thinking. As in the discourses of cultural racism, the cultural talk at UHS reinforced hegemonic ideas regarding race and American-ness. An emphasis on *cultural deficiency* simply extended this logic to include an explicit judgment of Hmong culture. Both the *cultural difference* and *cultural deficiency* perspectives were used to relieve the school from the responsibility of serving and/or recognizing the specific needs of Hmong American students. In both discourses, whiteness/middle class-ness remained the unspoken yet pervasive norm against which others were judged. Hmong American students were seen either as *culturally different* (i.e., foreign) or *culturally deficient* (i.e., like Blacks) when compared to the white norm. Both characterizations served to reflect and preserve the normative nature of whiteness and maintain the existing racial hierarchy. Located as outsiders, many Hmong American students were academically and socially marginalized at the school.

Hmong American students were well aware of the fact that the Hmong culture was not truly respected by the school. Many students complained that teachers and other members of the UHS staff view the Hmong culture as being inferior to "American" culture (i.e., White middle-class culture). Perhaps the most insidious influence of the culture of whiteness was that it led Hmong American students at UHS to internalize the implicit message that Whites are the only "real" Americans, as evidenced in their reserving the term "American" to refer to White people, while using ethnically or racially specific terms to identify themselves and other people of color. Second-generation students referred to themselves as "Americanized" Hmong, but they did not refer to themselves simply as "Americans." The association of American-ness with whiteness was confirmed by the popular culture. When I asked Hmong American students to describe "Americans," they described White people, often the stereotypic blue-eyed and blond White person. Furthermore, they asserted that "Americans" are rich, speak English, celebrate Christmas, and eat "American" food (e.g., pizza, hot dogs, and hamburgers). In short, when they spoke about "Americans" and "American culture," they typically described what they saw on TV and much of what they saw valued at UHS. Chapters 3 and 4 will focus on the various identities that Hmong American students create in response to and within this school culture.

3

"Traditional" and "Americanized" Hmong Students

The good kid will go back to the culture, whether it's a boy or a girl. When they come back home, they will, I guess, help the parents doing housework, chores. I guess dress differently, too, as a normal kid. And practicing some traditional culture. And going to school, attending school, getting good grades will be a good, a good child, a good boy or girl. And also, I guess doing what the parents want them to do . . . And, so the opposite is when the kids start to rebel or talk back to the parents, not obeying. And then wearing the baggy clothes, not attending school. Those are the bad kids.

Mrs. Her, Hmong bilingual resource specialist

Adults in the Hmong American community see their youth as falling into two distinct groups: "traditional" and "Americanized." Traditional youth are defined as those who have preserved their cultures and are therefore "good" kids. On the other hand, Americanized youth are defined as those who have "lost their culture" and turned into "bad" kids. Unlike many UHS teachers, who perceive the Hmong culture to be a barrier to school success and who assume that assimilation into the dominant culture is in the best interests of the Hmong American community, Hmong parents believe that the Hmong culture has a positive influence on their children and that assimilation is dangerous.

Like other immigrant parents in the United States, Hmong American adults view the forces of Americanization as the biggest threat to their children and families (Gibson, 1988; Valenzuela, 1999; Waters, 1999; Zhou & Bankston, 1998). In several studies Hmong parents have consistently expressed concerns about the threat of Americanization among Hmong youth (Donnelly, 1994; Faderman & Xiong, 1998). In an oral history of Hmong refugees, Faderman and Xiong (1998) found that Hmong parents

blame the schools in America: for undermining their authority by conflating discipline with child abuse, for failing to inculcate in children the moral feeling of guilt when they behave badly, for teaching their children things the parents regard as outrageous, such as sex education, which, the parents fear, will ruin their children for traditional Hmong life. (p. 13)

In meetings with UHS staff, Hmong parents regularly complained about the impact of Americanization on their teens. At a school district–sponsored meeting on gang awareness, Hmong mothers and fathers asserted that American laws regarding child abuse had taken away their right to use culturally specific means of controlling their children. Parents feared that if they even raised a hand to slap or spank their children they would be arrested for child abuse. Hmong adults asserted that youth who have lost their "traditional ways" were most at risk for gang activity. When the mayor of Lakeview called a meeting with Lakeview's Southeast Asian leaders to discuss the concerns of their community, several Hmong men reported that among the Hmong community's top fears are that their children are becoming "too Americanized" and that they are "losing control" of their children.

While it may sound as if Hmong adults were encouraging their children to reject all aspects of Americanization, my data suggest that Hmong adults were resisting aspects of Americanization that they viewed as either unnecessary for mainstream success or detrimental to mainstream success. Hmong adults were, for example, fearful that their children might adopt aspects of Americanization that might get them into trouble with the dominant group. Behaviors associated with delinquency were frequently referred to simply as Americanization. On the other hand, most Hmong immigrant parents supported the adoption of certain mainstream values or practices that were referred to as "good" Americanization. In short, most Hmong adults support the practice of accommodation without assimilation or selective acculturation (Gibson, 1988; Portes & Rumbaut, 2001). Thus the term *Americanized* worked as a floating signifier that shifted according to context. In short, Hmong adults want their children to do well in school and achieve economic success in mainstream society, but they also want them to maintain their Hmong culture and identity.

"TWO GROUPS OF HMONG STUDENTS"

During my first week at UHS Mrs. Her, one of the Hmong bilingual resource specialists, informed me that there were basically two groups of Hmong students at UHS. As a member of Lakeview's Hmong American community, Mrs. Her had an insider's perspective on how Hmong adults view their youth. Using diplomatic language, she referred to one group as the "newcomers" or ESL students and the other group as the "Americanized" students. According to Mrs. Her, ESL students obey their parents, work hard in school, dress conservatively, stay out of trouble, and are generally "more traditional." Mrs. Her explained that the "Americanized" students had adopted "American" styles of dress and behavior. She elaborated that Americanized kids challenge the authority of their parents, skip school and wear "gang"-type clothes. Mrs. Her suggested that the fact that most ESL students did not come to the United States until they were in elementary or middle school helped them to maintain their "traditional" ways. She also assumed that the American born status of "Americanized" youth explained their behavior.

My observations confirmed Mrs. Her's assertions regarding the relationship between generation and identity type. Most "traditional" students had arrived in the United States during elementary or middle school and are members of what some sociologists refer to as the 1.5-generation, and all "Americanized" students were born in the United States, making them members of the second generation (Portes, 1996; Rumbaut, 1991).

Although Mrs. Her is careful not to mention race, gang-style clothing is associated with urban youth of color. Like many of the teachers in Valenzuela's (1999) study on Mexican American high school students, Mrs. Her assumed that youth who wear urban-style clothing are delinquents who do not care about school. Mrs. Her went on to explain that Americanized kids were the ones with whom UHS encountered difficulties.

> We don't have problems with those ESL kids. Because, they are, I don't know, they seem, maybe they're not Americanized or you know, so they are still, . . . let's say, good kids. So they are working hard and trying to graduate from UHS. The other problems, I think the problem that most of the Hmong students face are students who are in the mainstream—they are facing truancy.

Mrs. Her asserted that during the 1980s, when most Hmong students at UHS were newcomers to the United States, there were few behavioral problems within the Hmong student community. What stands out here is that "Americanized" (i.e., second-generation) students are the ones described as having problems in school. Like many recent scholars of immigration (Rumbaut & Portes, 2001; Valenzuela, 1999; Waters, 1999; Zhou & Bankston, 1998), Mrs. Her links Americanization with poor school achievement. It is important to point out, however, that the Americanization that Mrs. Her deemed dangerous is the kind associated with poor people of color.

Like Hmong adults, Hmong American students at UHS used the terms "traditional" and "Americanized" to describe themselves and each other. The remainder of this chapter will examine the way traditional and Americanized students construct their identities as Hmong at UHS. The focus will be on the way each group negotiates their identities in response to school experiences, messages from the dominant society, and relationships with the Hmong community. In particular, I will examine the way their experiences negotiating race inform their identities as Hmong. I will also explore how traditional and Americanized youths' identities as students are formed through their relationship with teachers, and intersect with their Hmong identities. Finally, I will focus on the ways students' identities as the children of immigrants inform their understandings of being Hmong at UHS and in the larger U.S. society.

CONSTRUCTING IDENTITIES AGAINST EACH OTHER

Research on identity formation suggests that groups define their identities in relation to those they identify as others (Barth, 1969; Hall, 1996; Proweller, 1998; Thorne, 1993). As Proweller (1998) notes, "identities are constituted along borders that separate who one is from who one is not" (p. 62). At UHS Americanized youth and traditional youth defined themselves against each other. What it meant to belong to one group was largely based on not being like the other group. From my research at UHS it seems that the social borders between the groups were rarely crossed at school. Traditional students and Americanized students rarely spoke to one another at school. Students in one group would admit to having cousins in the other group, but they maintained their distance at school. They sat at different tables in the cafeteria. They wore different styles of clothes. While the traditional students were in ESL, most Americanized students have been mainstreamed at UHS after having spent years in ESL during elementary and middle school.

Of the Hmong students who participated in extracurricular activities, the traditional students joined the school's Asian Club, while many of the Americanized students joined the school's Hmong Cultural Club. The most significant exception to this pattern was an Americanized male who was the president of the Asian Club during the 1998–99 academic year. This student, like the other members of the Asian Club, had a distinctly proschool attitude. The Asian Club included both American-born and foreign-born Asian American students from various ethnic groups (e.g., Chinese, Tibetan, Hmong, Vietnamese, and Indian). Members of this club were interested in teaching non-Asians about their various cultures. All of the active members of the Hmong Cultural Club were second-generation Hmong American students, most of whom could be described as being American-ized. Compared to the Asian Club, the members of the Hmong Cultural Club had a more explicitly social agenda. Students were interested in organizing dances, taking field trips to amusement parks, and watching videos.

I was initially surprised to find that the traditional Hmong American youth did not participate in the Hmong Cultural Club, but traditional youth informed me that their decision to be in the Asian Club was based on their desire to avoid associating with the Americanized youth. The traditional students reported that their parents warned them to stay away from "bad kids" who were "too Americanized." Echoing the sentiments of the pa-rental generation, one self-defined traditional student compared the two groups like this: "We are more traditional. We speak Hmong and know the Hmong culture. The others speak more English—they want to be cool. They don't follow what adults say."

Although traditional youth were careful to distance themselves from Americanized youth, the Americanized youth were even more intent on highlighting the differences between the two groups. Americanized youth ridiculed traditional students for being too traditional, conservative, and old-fashioned. They used derogatory terms such as "FOB" or "FOBBIES" (i.e., Fresh Off the Boat) to describe traditional students. One American-ized student described traditional students like this: "FOBs don't care about clothes. They are stingy about clothes. They dress in out-of-date 1980s-style clothes. American-born Hmong are into clothes and cars." Like other immigrant youth, the Americanized youth had learned that consumer-ism was a sign of American-ness, and they were quick to wear their signs of American-ness (Olsen, 1997; Zhou & Bankston, 1998). For the Ameri-canized youth, the traditional youth represent the foreign identity from which they want to distance themselves. Their experiences at UHS and in the larger society had taught them that an immigrant status was a stigma-tized status. By disparaging traditional youth, the Americanized youth were casting out the aspects of the Hmong community they viewed as prob-lematic for life in the United States. Other researchers have identified a similar antipathy between American-born ethnics and their foreign-born peers (Valenzuela, 1999; Verma, 2004).

The fact that traditional and Americanized students formed and de-fined their respective identities in opposition to each other reflects their awareness that Hmong adults constantly compare the two groups. Fur-thermore, the focus on intra-ethnic differences between traditional and Americanized youth reflects their understanding that members of the dominant group tend to see all Hmong students as being the same, a fact that each group is resisting. It is important to note that while Hmong

American youth focused a great deal of attention on intra-ethnic differences, they were also cognizant of other ethnic and racial groups. As I will illustrate in this chapter, Americanized and traditional youth were acutely aware that racial groups held differing levels of power and status at the school and in the larger U.S. society, and they formed their identities in response to their perceptions of the racial hierarchy.

Reflecting the largely Black-and-White discourse surrounding race in the United States, Americanized and traditional students focused their attention on White and Black students. Other immigrants have been found to construct their identities in relation to the largely Black-and-White discourse on race in the United States (Lee, 1996; Park, 1997; Waters, 1999). Park (1997), for example, found that Korean immigrants were aware that they possess a lower status than Whites, but they view their status in relation to Blacks to be more ambiguous. Similarly, traditional and Americanized Hmong students at UHS recognized that they lacked the status and privileges of Whites. Both groups viewed Whites as the only authentic Americans.

"TRADITIONAL" HMONG YOUTH: THE 1.5 GENERATION

During lunch hours, traditional students could be found sitting in the cafeteria with other foreign-born Asians they knew through ESL classes. Traditional students can be heard switching back and forth between Hmong and English. Most report that they are more comfortable speaking Hmong, but like to speak in English. The English they speak is the rather formal English learned primarily in an academic context. Typical topics of conversation during lunchtime include family and school.

Traditional students are largely optimistic about life in the United States. Those who remember life before coming to the United States stress that things are better here than in their native countries. According to many scholars, this "dual frame of reference" is typical of immigrant children and allows them to persist in the face of difficulties in the new country (Ogbu, 1987; Suarez-Orozco, 1989). Students of both genders assert that there are greater educational opportunities in the United States than in Laos or Thailand.

ESL as a Safe Space

Most of the traditional Hmong students are enrolled in the school's English as a Second Language program. While Hmong students represented a significant portion of the ESL population in the 1980s and early 1990s, the number of Hmong students had declined by the late 1990s. The ESL program offers courses in reading and language skills, social studies, science, math, and business. Students making the transition from ESL to mainstream classes are also offered a course in guided study. During the 1998–99 academic year the program included five teachers and a few part-time bilingual resource specialists, including one Hmong speaker. A second Hmong bilingual resource specialist was hired during the 1999–2000 academic year to work with Hmong students who were experiencing academic difficulties. The educational backgrounds of bilingual resource specialists vary, but all must demonstrate that they are bilingual in English and Spanish, Chinese, or Hmong. The responsibilities of the bilingual resource specialists include: tutoring ESL students; assisting ESL teachers; translating and interpreting communication between home and school; and meeting with parents to provide information about their child's education. Finally, the school employs a bilingual guidance counselor who helps ESL students select courses and make other educational decisions.

Ms. Heinemann, a 25-year veteran of the Lakeview District, was the chair of the ESL program during the 1998–99 school year. She explained that the ESL program serves students from over 20 different language backgrounds. According to Ms. Heinemann, the mission of ESL at UHS is to teach English language learners the academic and cultural skills to make the transition to mainstream classes. She explained, "I think we're teaching language and culture, including the culture of an American high school and how to access that." She offers ESL students explicit instruction in cultural skills and language skills.

In her classes Ms. Heinemann introduces students to various aspects of the dominant society that are necessary for mainstream success. She makes explicit the tacit cultural norms of the school and the larger society. One day in her advanced ESL class, for example, Ms. Heinemann discussed nonverbal communication in the United States.

> Standing at the front of the room, Ms. Heinemann demonstrated various nonverbal gestures. Staring at one student, she asked, "What does staring mean?" A student responded by saying that staring is rude, and Ms. Heinemann nodded. Yawning, she asked, "What does it mean? What does it mean if you yawn in class?" Next, she averted her eyes and asked, "Is it negative or positive for student–teacher and teacher–student interactions if a student does not make eye contact?" She explained that while eye contact is considered inappropriate in some cultures, teachers in the United States appreciate eye contact. She used her experiences traveling abroad to illustrate cultural differences in nonverbal communica-

tion. She smiled and noted that she found that "Americans smile at strangers more than other people." She then asked students to compare nonverbal communication patterns in the United States with patterns in their own countries.

Field note, 3/10/99

As Delpit (1988) argues, poor children and children of color "must be taught the codes needed to participate fully in the mainstream of American life" while they are also encouraged "to acknowledge their own 'expertness' as well" (p. 296). Ms. Heinemann did exactly that in her advanced ESL classroom. By explicitly telling students that teachers appreciate eye contact from their students, Ms. Heinemann gave students a rule of the culture of power (Delpit, 1988). Although she introduced mainstream American styles of nonverbal communication to her students, she demonstrated respect for styles of nonverbal communication common to the students' native cultures.

A consistent theme in Ms. Heinemann's classes was a respect for cultural differences. She regularly asked students to share information about their cultural backgrounds. Although English was the sole language of instruction in her classes, she gave students opportunities to use their native languages. On some days, for example, she put the students into same-language groups to complete assignments and instructed them to use their native languages to help each other. On other days she instructed students to form groups with speakers of other languages so they would have to communicate in English.

In addition to addressing issues related to culture, Ms. Heinemann focused on teaching students the academic skills necessary for mainstream classes. She made concerted efforts to align the ESL curriculum with the curriculum in mainstream classes so that the transition from ESL to mainstream classes would be relatively seamless. In short, she recognized that ESL students must be held to high academic standards if they are to succeed in mainstream classes.

Although the ESL program at UHS includes culturally sensitive professionals like Ms. Heinemann, the program has its share of problems. I spoke with ESL teachers who appeared to view students' native cultures and languages as barriers to be overcome. One ESL teacher, for example, posted a sign on his door that read "ENGLISH ONLY SPOKEN HERE." The implicit message here was that students' native languages are a hindrance to learning English. This same teacher relied on worksheets that asked students to regurgitate information from lectures or textbooks. He gave multiple-choice exams that asked students to choose the one right answer without opportunity for critical analysis or writing. Traditional students described this teacher as being "nice, but too easy." Unfortunately, time spent in this teacher's ESL class did not prepare students for mainstream classes at UHS that required class discussion and extensive written work. In short, the curriculum and pedagogy in his class reflected the problems common in many ESL classes and in lower-track classrooms (Oakes, 1985; Page, 1991; Valdes, 2001).

Another problem with the ESL program at UHS is that it isolated and segregated ESL students from mainstream students. ESL students at UHS, like those at other schools, had few opportunities to interact with native English speakers. As many have argued, it is difficult for English-language learners to become fluent in English when they are completely segregated from their native-English-speaking peers (Olsen, 1997; Tse, 2001; Valdes, 2001). Well aware of the isolating environment of ESL, Ms. Heinemann has made efforts to build relationships between the ESL department and mainstream departments. She believes that ESL students can derive both academic and social benefits from opportunities to interact with native-English-speaking students.

> I'm very concerned about holding kids separate, because for their learning they need to be in contact with peers. And I think for our society, if we don't have different groups mixing at the high school level, some of those groups will never mix. So, for those two reasons, I've worked really hard to try to create joint courses between departments.

Despite the efforts of the ESL program to integrate ESL students into the mainstream of the school, however, ESL and former ESL students remain socially segregated from mainstream students.

A few ESL teachers also expressed concern that students were being trapped in ESL. Ms. Cohen, a new member of the ESL staff in 1999, pointed out that students who spent their high school careers in ESL rarely ended up taking advanced classes like calculus. Ms. Cohen and Ms. Heinemann suggested that the increasingly difficult standards for exiting ESL programs that had been adopted by the school district were partly to blame. They also pointed out that when former ESL students struggled in their mainstream classes they were often sent back to ESL. Similarly, Valdes (2001) found that mainstream teachers "were especially reluctant to have non-English-background students in their classes no matter what levels of proficiency they had reached" (p. 36).

Ms. Heinemann and other ESL staff asserted that they have tried to address the problems in the ESL program, but they have found their efforts thwarted by the lack of resources and by school district regulations. Like many school districts around the country, the Lakeview School District has struggled to serve the fast-growing ESL population. The cost of educating the ESL population and the struggle to find qualified ESL teachers are two issues facing the district. In the 1992–93 academic year there were just 809 students identified by the school district as limited English proficiency (LEP). By the 1998–99 school year there were 1,571 LEP students, and by 1999–2000 there were 1,889 LEP students. In 2002 there were approximately 2,800 LEP students in the district. During the 2001–02 academic year the state of Wisconsin reimbursed the school district 16 cents on the dollar for LEP expenses.

Despite these problems, most of the traditional students in ESL describe the program as a safe space in an otherwise large and intimidating school. These students explained that in their ESL classes they are afforded the freedom to develop their English-language skills without fear of being ridiculed by mainstream students (Olsen, 1997; Tse, 2001). Many of these students report having close relationships with their ESL teachers, which confirms their faith in the American educational system. Significantly, the most respected teachers are those who know something about the students' lives outside of school. These teachers take the time to learn about their students' cultures, and they provide their students with information about academic and nonacademic issues.

Ms. Heinemann, for example, has helped students with income taxes. She regularly works with the school nurse to help students deal with health related concerns. In addressing issues related to family and health, Ms. Heinemann moved beyond the "public" and "private" dichotomy that characterizes the position taken by many educators and educational institutions (Fine, 1991; Valenzuela, 1999). In short, Ms. Heinemann understands that how students perform at school (i.e., the public sphere) is influenced by what happens in their families and communities (i.e., the private sphere).

Traditional students also identified Mrs. Her as a supportive and knowledgeable adult at UHS. In her role as a Hmong bilingual resource specialist, Mrs. Her had regular contact with many of the Hmong families and therefore understood the specific context of traditional students' lives. As a Hmong immigrant, Mrs. Her shared with traditional students the experience of adjusting to a new country and the belief that the United States offered great educational opportunities for all.

Finally, in addition to positive relationships with ESL staff, many ESL students viewed Mr. Buckner, the AHANA coordinator, as a trusted adult figure at the school.

Perceptions of Education

As I noted in the previous section, traditional Hmong American students' positive experiences in the ESL program confirmed their positive attitudes regarding education. These students have a "folk theory of success" that links education to social mobility (Ogbu, 1987, 1992). Traditional students dream of attending college or vocational school after they graduate from high school because they believe that education is the route to ascending the socioeconomic ladder of the American society. Furthermore, these students feel indebted to their parents for the sacrifices they have made for the family, and they feel obligated to repay their parents by working hard in school. This motivation for school achievement has been identified among immigrants from many cultures (Gibson, 1988; Suarez-Orozco, 1989; Suarez-Orozco & Suarez-Orozco, 2001; Waters, 1999).

It is not uncommon to find members of the traditional students studying in groups before school and during lunch. The highest-achieving students seek out other hard-working foreign born Asians as friends and study companions. Friendly competition over test scores on the latest French or chemistry test helps to further motivate the students. Many traditional students are well aware that UHS has a reputation for being an excellent school with high academic standards. In comparing UHS to schools in Thailand or Laos, they conclude that the educational opportunities in the United States are far superior and feel fortunate to be attending such a school. In short, traditional students express a great deal of optimism regarding life in the United States, and school is at the center of their dreams for the future.

The majority of traditional students work hard and pass their classes. A few students achieve high levels of academic success, as evidenced by their places on the honor roll. Although the majority of these students pass their classes, a few students fall into a pattern of chronic truancy. The Hmong bilingual resource specialists explained that some students begin skipping classes because they can't keep up with the material. According to Mr. Thao, one of the Hmong bilingual resource specialists, some students are overlooked because they are quiet, and teachers assume that they are making progress. Here, the stereotype of the hard-working, quiet model minority emerges and works against the students' best interest.

Other chronic truants, however, have come to the attention of school authorities for engaging in "negative behaviors." Sam, for example, began skipping classes because he couldn't understand the material. Since becoming a chronic truant, he has been suspended for fighting on more than one occasion. According to the 10th-grade principal, the most recent suspension came after Sam punched a White student for calling him a derogatory name. Although the principal was sympathetic to Sam, he could not make exceptions to the rules regarding fighting. For Sam, the suspension served to confirm his suspicions that UHS is a racist institution. Although Sam did not socialize with the Americanized students, Mr. Thao thought of Sam as an Americanized student. Mr. Thao suggested that Sam's problems in school were related to his "becoming Americanized," and he appeared to view Sam as being beyond help.

Social Isolation

As stated earlier, traditional students primarily socialized with students in the ESL program. In the cafeteria, traditional students sat at tables near students who appeared to be loners and students in the special education program. Both the ESL students and the loners wear relatively nondescript clothes and sit relatively quietly, thereby blending into their surroundings. The fact that traditional students sat in close proximity to the loners and the special education students reflects the marginalized status of ESL students at the school (Gitlin et al, 2003). In short, traditional students appear to be largely invisible to the larger student population.

Interestingly, the only complaint traditional Hmong American students consistently expressed about UHS concerned the social environment of the school and the isolation of ESL students. In my observations, I found that traditional students rarely had contact with White or African American students. Traditional students explained that they wanted to get to know "American" (read: White) students, but "American" students appeared to be uninterested in getting to know them. In an exasperated tone, Zoua, a traditional student, asserted, "It is frustrating that Americans don't want to be friends." Another traditional student declared, "Americans are snobs."

When I asked Zoua and her friends why they believed they had difficulty getting to know American students, they pointed to their own limitations with the English language. Like other recent immigrants, traditional students continue to hold on to some hope that English language fluency will grant them full incorporation into American society (Olsen, 1997). Some traditional students were beginning to suspect that being in ESL carried a social stigma that might limit their opportunities to befriend Americans. Not insignificantly, traditional students vehemently denied the role of racism in their social isolation. Zoua, however, did say that "prejudice" on the part of "ignorant people" could play a role.

In my conversations with traditional students I was struck by the fact that while they were bothered about being ignored by Whites, they did not appear concerned about the social distance between themselves and African American students. Initially I assumed that traditional students' preoccupation with Whites simply reflected their recognition that Whites have economic, political, and social power in the United States. Subsequently I learned that some traditional students have formed negative opinions about African Americans. Although I never heard traditional students voice any negative opinions about African Americans, Ms. Heinemann expressed some anxiety that ESL students, including some Hmong students, held prejudicial attitudes toward African Americans. Recent research on other immigrant groups reveals similar patterns of prejudice toward African Americans (Waters, 1999). I would suggest that the traditional students' attitudes toward Whites and African Americans demonstrate that newcomers quickly recognize the existence of the racial hierarchy.

Family Obligations

A common phenomenon in immigrant families involves the role reversal between immigrant parents and their children whereby the children must help their parents navigate the new society (Kibria, 1993; Portes & Rumbaut, 1996; Song, 1999; Suarez-Orozco & Sung, 1987; Waters, 1999). In her work on Chinese immigrants in Britain, for example, Song (1999) found that male and female children perform a variety of "caring work" for their immigrant parents. Because the children of immigrants often possess greater English-language skills than their parents, they frequently become responsible for interpreting for their parents, translating documents, and paying bills. Forced to take on adult responsibilities, the children of immigrants have little time to engage in the activities associated with middle-class U.S. teen life.

Most of the traditional Hmong youth at UHS report having significant family responsibilities that they must juggle along with their studies. Like other children from immigrant families, Hmong students at UHS are responsible for interpreting for their parents, driving their parents to appointments, performing various household chores, and even working to help support the family (Portes & Rumbaut, 1996; Song, 1999). Many Hmong youth also report that they are expected to help tend the family vegetable gardens. During the summer elementary-age children and high school–age youth accompany their parents to farmers' markets, where they sell produce from the family garden.

Each of the traditional Hmong American students in my study had stories about helping their parents. Jackson, a senior in high school, is the only driver in his family and is therefore responsible for chauffeuring his parents and siblings to various appointments. Occasionally he misses classes because his parents have to go to the doctor during school hours. Cha, a sophomore, worked every night at a local supermarket in order to earn money to help support his mother, who is on disability. Girls, in particular, are expected to help cook, clean, and take care of younger siblings. May, a sophomore, wakes up at 6:15 A.M. and helps her younger siblings get ready for school. She catches the bus at 7:00 and meets her friends to study in the school cafeteria for an hour before school starts. After a full day of academic classes, she attends Upward Bound until 7:00 P.M. When she gets home, she cooks dinner and then helps her siblings with their homework before doing her own homework. By the time she goes to bed at midnight she is exhausted. Jackson, Cha, May, and others perform this caring work because they feel obligated to their parents and because they believe that helping their parents is part of being traditional youth. Despite the fact that the traditional parent–child relationships are reversed within these families, parental authority is preserved.

Weddings and funerals are examples of other family/cultural obligations that occupy traditional and Americanized Hmong American students' time. It is not uncommon, for example, for students to miss several days of school in order to travel out of state to attend the funeral of a relative. Not insignificantly, family obligations can interfere with students' educational pursuits. In her research on Hmong college students, for example, Ngo (2000) discovered that students often had to choose between their education and their family responsibilities. Traditional students rarely complained about attending family events because they viewed participation in these events as central family obligations.

The Politics of Being Traditional

Descriptions of ESL students as "not Americanized" and "traditional" suggest a kind of cultural purity. Although Mrs. Her and other Hmong adults described ESL students as being "traditionally Hmong," it would be a mistake to assume that traditional students' expressions of being Hmong are identical to the ways of being Hmong in Laos. Despite the fact that these students are described as adhering to traditional values, the Hmong culture has not remained static or fixed. It would be more accurate to describe traditional youth as engaging in very selective acculturation. Even as relative newcomers, 1.5 generation/traditional students and their families have made cultural adjustments in response to life in the United States. Like other immigrants, Hmong parents are fully aware of the importance of English in the United States, and as such they encourage their children to become fluent in English as quickly as possible. One of the biggest of these adjustments is their increased support for the education of girls and women (Goldstein, 1985; Koltyk, 1998; Lee, 1997). Furthermore, it is important to point out that while traditional students may obey their parents' rules out of respect, this does not mean that they do not question Hmong cultural norms. Some "traditional" youth asserted that that they will raise their own children in "Hmong and American ways." May, for example, asserted that she would teach her children to value gender equality. Such attitudes suggest a more complex embracing of Hmong culture than evidenced at first glance.

When students describe themselves as being "traditional," they are saying as much or more about what they are not (i.e., Americanized) as what they are. These students are not rejecting all values associated with being American or Americanized, but they are rejecting the behaviors associated with the Americanized youth. In fact, they are embracing certain aspects of mainstream American culture (e.g., support for formal education) and renaming them as traditional Hmong values. The flexibility of Hmong culture to respond to social and political forces is the reason that Hmong culture has endured ethnic minority status in Laos, war, refugee camps, and relocation (Dunnigan, 1986; Fish, 1991; Hendricks, 1986).

By describing "good kids" as "traditional," the Hmong American youth and adults are reclaiming pride in their culture. They are resisting the dominant group's characterization of Hmong culture as backward and otherwise problematic. Like other immigrants of color, Hmong Americans have to deal with the dominant group's cultural insensitivity and pressures to assimilate. By emphasizing aspects of their culture that mainstream Americans value (e.g., respect for elders), and deemphasizing aspects of Hmong culture considered to be problematic (e.g., early marriage), members of the Hmong community are strategically developing their public face (Koltyk, 1998; Kurien, 1999). In an effort to gain acceptance, they are attempting to build an identity as a model minority (Kurien, 1999; Lee, 1996; Waters, 1999). Koltyk (1998) made a similar observation in her research:

> To manage a positive image, one devoid of the kind of sensationalism created by the media, many Hmong resort to strategies of censorship, restricting outsiders' access to certain information and cultural practices, while at the same time developing overt displays of tradition that are cast in ways that are acceptable to the dominant group. (p. 14)

Central to the construction of this public face is the claim that educational persistence and achievement are linked to traditional Hmong values. By blaming Americanization for corrupting their youth, the Hmong community is redirecting any negative criticism of Hmong youth away from the Hmong culture.

"AMERICANIZED" HMONG YOUTH:
THE SECOND GENERATION

> For the young, there is no going back. For better or worse, they are Americans. (Faderman & Xiong, 1998, p. 88)

During the lunch period, large groups of "Americanized" Hmong students gather at tables in the cafeteria. While all Americanized Hmong students are welcome, the students they refer to as "FOBs" are not. As noted in chapter 2, second-generation Hmong students do not feel as though they are accepted as true and authentic Americans. In negotiating their identities, most second-generation Hmong students focus on the process of being Americanized, as defined and made available through popular and consumer cultures. Thus, these students are attempting to distance themselves from the foreigner image that haunts Hmong and other Asian Americans. As stated previously, Americanized youth perceive the process of Americanization as requiring and achieving social distance from traditional Hmong youth.

For the majority of Americanized youth, the process of Americanization includes adopting the hip-hop style associated with urban youth of color. The young men wear baggy pants and oversized T-shirts and have either long hair or shortly shorn hair. The young women wear baggy pants or hip-hugging bell-bottoms with short tops that show off their mid-riffs. Many of the Americanized youth work at clothing stores in the mall or at discount clothing stores so that they can buy fashionable clothes at a discount. Most Americanized youth report being more comfortable speaking English than Hmong. The English they speak is peppered with hip-hop terms and occasional Hmong phrases. Students listen to hip-hop, pop, and rap music performed by Hmong American, African American, and White recording artists. The fact that most Americanized students have adopted a hip-hop style has contributed to their blackening in the dominant imagination.

Americanized youth enjoy attending Hmong soccer and volleyball tournaments, where they socialize with other Hmong youth and purchase CDs and videos featuring Hmong and other Asian artists. Many spend their weekends traveling to cities throughout the Midwest to attend these tournaments. There were a few hundred young people at the tournament I attended, and my informants informed me that it was one of the smaller tournaments. Americanized students reported that tournaments were good places to meet people to date and to find out about the latest music.

Interpreting Race

In contrast to the generally hopeful attitude of the 1.5 generation, most second-generation students are somewhat cynical about life in the United States because of ongoing experiences with poverty and racism. Second-generation/Americanized students complained that non-Hmong people mock their culture and stereotype them as lazy welfare recipients with big families. Students told stories about being treated like gang members by store clerks, police officers, and others. Like other youth of color, Americanized Hmong American youth are criminalized in the dominant imagination (Cammarato, 2004; Ferguson, 2000; Vo & Danico, 2004; Waters, 1999). Some Americanized youth responded to the racial harassment and suspicions by playing on the fears of the dominant group. One Americanized female student explained:

> Sometimes we always have fun if we go to the store. And I am like getting off of the subject, but sometimes when you go to the store and we just dress like we do—wear baggy pants and stuff and people are like looking at us like we are going to steal something. So we kind of make fun of that. We tend to act suspicious. We make the salespeople really nervous. We always go in the changing room to make us look suspicious. It is really funny. I do that sometimes, 'cause I get really pissed when they look at us like that, but I don't steal.

This student added that she had money and didn't need to steal. Her reference to having money appeared to be a response to the stereotype that Hmong Americans are welfare-dependent. This student and other Americanized students noted that White people were the ones most likely to stereotype them as welfare recipients and gangsters. The fact that African Americans are also stereotyped as welfare recipients and gang members suggests how closely Hmong Americans are positioned to African Americans in the racial hierarchy.

At UHS White students and Hmong American students occupied separate spaces and had little meaningful contact. While Hmong American students ate in the cafeteria because they were on reduced-price or free lunch, most White students, particularly upper-level students, avoided the cafeteria. Americanized Hmong students and White students participated in different extracurricular activities. Although Americanized Hmong students were in classes with White students, and occasionally engaged in brief conversations with White students, these contacts did not lead to friendships. The one notable exception to this pattern was a friendship between a few Americanized female students who were chronic truants and a White female student who was also a chronic truant. Unfortunately, I did not have an opportunity to interview this particular young White woman, but in my observations I noticed that she was treated like an honorary member of the Americanized Hmong crowd, particularly by students who were the most alienated from school. Many of the Americanized youth appeared to view this student as being different from other Whites, and on more than one occasion I heard Americanized students joking about giving this student a Hmong name.

Despite this one friendship, my observations suggest that Hmong American students recognized that they were largely invisible to the majority of White students. As with immigrant students in other studies, the relative invisibility of Hmong American youth at UHS reflected their low status at the school (Hall, 2002; Olsen, 1997). One instance, in particular, demonstrates that Americanized youth felt ignored by their White peers. During one lunch period members of the Hmong Cultural Club were discussing plans for a Hmong Cultural Club dance. The goal of the dance was to earn money for an end-of-the-year trip for club members. As the members discussed plans for publicity, they complained that "American" (read: White) students never attend Hmong dances. One student suggested that in the posters advertising the dance that the word "Hmong" should simply be omitted. They all agreed that the dance would most likely draw a crowd if they didn't mention the word "Hmong." I asked the students whether posters for previous dances had made it clear that the dance was open to everyone, and they all nodded affirmatively. According to these Americanized students, White students were simply uninterested in attending Hmong events, and uninterested in socializing with Hmong American students.

The invisibility of Hmong American students did not mean they were free from the judgment of their non-Hmong peers. As Rita's comments in chapter 2 suggested, some non-Hmong students have begun to stereotype Hmong students as gang members. Americanized students were sensitive to the ways White students viewed them. They were acutely aware that aspects of the Hmong culture were frowned upon by the dominant society, particularly White people. On one occasion, while sitting with a group of Americanized girls in the cafeteria, I overheard a group of White girls at another table talking about an article they were reading in a teen magazine about a family of 10 or so children. As the White girls laughed at the size of the family, one of the Americanized girls muttered under her breath that she was from a big family. Experiences like this have led most Americanized youth to distrust and distance themselves from their White peers.

Sia, a graduate of the class of 1999, describes her experiences with White people in the following quote:

> For me, I feel, I just feel like some White people neglect me. I mean as much as I try to be nice to them, give them respect, they don't give it back to me. Why should I even bother with them? Because I feel like I really don't need people like that. . . . I mean, if you're not Asian like me, you don't understand where I'm coming from either. Like White people, I mean, they may say they do, but I don't see it. They don't really know how it feels.

Through their experiences with Whites, Sia and her friends have concluded that they cannot trust White people.

Significantly, Sia's distrust of White people extends to her distrust of White teachers. While traditional students assume that the social distance between Whites and Hmong are rooted in language differences, Americanized students point to issues of race and culture. While many traditional students respond to racism by redirecting their focus to the positive aspects of life in the United States, Americanized students are understandably unwilling to overlook instances of racism and discrimination. As members of the second generation, Americanized youth do not have a dual frame of reference (Suarez-Orozco & Suarez-Orozco, 2001). They are more likely to compare themselves to their White middle-class peers than to relatives in Thailand or Laos. All they know is life in the United States, and they want to be treated like real Americans.

While the relationship between most Americanized youth and Whites could be characterized as distant and distrustful, the relationship between Americanized youth and African Americans was more ambiguous. Previous research has highlighted the interracial tensions between African Americans and Southeast Asian Americans (Lee, 1996; Lei, 2003). In my earlier research, for example, I found that the characterization of Southeast Asian American students as model minorities was used against African Americans and contributed to the tensions between the two groups. While I did not observe any friendships between African American students and Hmong American students at UHS, I also did not observe overt expressions of animosity between the groups. Americanized students and most African American students lived in the poorer areas of Lakeview. Americanized students grew up next to African American families and therefore had a familiarity with African Americans that they did not have with Whites.

Americanized youth recognized that both Hmong Americans and African Americans were beneath Whites in the social hierarchy of UHS and the larger society. Although they saw that some African American students at UHS gained some status through sports and other extracurricular activities, they recognized that the highest status went to White students. Their understanding of the position of African Americans in the racial hierarchy informed their responses to African Americans. For instance, Sia stated that when African Americans fail to treat her with respect it does not bother her as much as when Whites mistreat her. She explained, "I don't let that disturb me. Because I can easily prove them wrong, you know." She went on to explain that while "White people are successful," African Americans were not more successful than Hmong people.

While Americanized youth viewed African Americans as economically and politically unsuccessful relative to Whites, they understood that hip-hop culture, which they associated with African Americans, had an oppositional social power and consumer power. Cultural critics have argued that hip-hop clothes, music, and language are, at least in part, about resistance to White mainstream culture (Kelley, 1997). It is this opposition to authority that attracted some Americanized youth to hip-hop culture. Of course, the oppositional politics of hip-hop culture appeal to some White youths as well. In a discussion of White middle-class youths' attraction to hip-hop, Kelley (1997) asserts, "Hip Hop, particularly gangsta rap, also attracts listeners for whom the 'ghetto' is a place of adventure, unbridled violence, erotic fantasy, and/or an imaginary alternative to suburban boredom" (p. 39).

In contrast to White middle-class youth, however, Americanized youth are marginalized along race and class lines. My data suggest that hip-hop style, for Americanized students, was a form of resistance to race and class exclusion. Americanized youth recognized that their clothes were read in racialized terms, and I found that several Americanized students described themselves as "dressing ghetto." The term "ghetto" was used in a defiant way and was implicitly associated African Americans. The use of the term "ghetto" to describe their style also seems to suggest that they identify with African Americans and against Whites. In other words, I argue that Americanized youth were consciously choosing styles that were not associated with White middle-class youth. I was informed by several Americanized males, for example, that the athletic jackets worn by students who lettered in a sport were "White boy jackets" and that they would never wear one even if they lettered in a sport.

At UHS many teachers assumed that the adoption of hip-hop style among Hmong American youth was a bad sign—an indication that they were Americanizing in bad ways, a sign that they were involved in gangs. While there were White students at UHS who adopted hip-hop styles, teachers did not appear to be concerned about what that meant. It is important to point out that while students embraced hip-hop style as an expression of oppositional identity, this style was not necessarily, as many teachers assumed, evidence of gang activity.

Although I argue that hip-hop style represented a political choice for many Americanized youth, other Americanized youth appeared to simply be following the styles chosen by the youth in their neighborhoods. Similarly, in her ethnographic study of racial identity among White high school students, Perry (2002) found that poor and working-class Whites who grew up in neighborhoods with African American youth had "commonalities of experience and dispositions that resulted in similar styles and ways of being" (p. 51). In these cases, taste in clothes and music are produced by both their class context (Bourdieu, 1984) and racial context (Kelley, 1997). Although Americanized youth acknowledged that their styles of speech and clothing were associated with African Americans, they were quick to point out that they were not Black.

Popular culture also played a significant role in Americanized students' attitudes toward African Americans and hip-hop culture. Hip-hop, more than other forms of popular culture, has reflected a fascination with an Asian aesthetic (Ho, 2004). Asian and Asian American celebrities have appeared in numerous movies with African American celebrities. During my fieldwork the movie *Romeo Must Die*, starring Jet Li and Aaliyah, was playing in theatres. Jet Li, the Chinese American martial artist and star of multiple action movies, was one of the Americanized youths' favorite celebrities. A hip-hop retelling of *Romeo and Juliet*, *Romeo Must Die* focused on two families, one Chinese American and one African American, fighting for control of the waterfront. Jet Li and Aaliyah, the African American hip-hop artist, played the Romeo and Juliet characters. The movie was extremely popular among the Americanized students, who identified Li, wearing hip-hop clothing, as an oppositional hero who defeated his enemies. While Jet Li brought in an Asian American youth audience, Aaliyah, who has been described as the Princess Diana of hip-hop, brought in an African American youth audience. That the movie appealed to a largely youth of color audience was not lost on the Americanized youth. One commented cheerfully, "Usually when we go to the movies it is mostly Americans there, but this time it was Asians and African Americans."

"I Hate Being Poor"

Like many traditional youth, many Americanized youth struggle with issues related to poverty. While traditional students remain generally hopeful that they will be able to overcome poverty, Americanized students' long-term experiences with poverty have left them relatively defeated. Moua Y., a senior in the class of 2000, spoke about her family's economic struggles. Her family moved to Wisconsin from California because they had heard there were greater economic opportunities in Wisconsin. Her father works two jobs, and her mother works one full-time job, takes in sewing on the side, and maintains a garden that provides vegetables for the family. During her senior year, Moua worked part-time on weekends to save money to attend community college. Her older brother worked nights and weekends throughout the last 2 years of high school. While her family does struggle by middle-class standards, they experience relative economic security when compared to many Hmong American families in Lakeview. Toua Vang's family, for example, has struggled financially since her father died unexpectedly a few years ago. Toua Vang lives with her mother and two siblings in low-income housing.

Based on their observations of White students at UHS and what they have gleaned from popular culture, Americanized youth conclude that most Whites are wealthy. Toua Vang said that she knew that White students have money because "they drive nice cars, wear nice clothes, and have their own cell phones." Moua imagines that the typical White family is economically well off and loving. She says:

> When I think of the mainstream I think of a White family, I guess. As both parents working . . . have really good jobs and maybe one kid or two kids, three at the most. And the kids are doing house chores and everything, they like have good grades and even when the girl grows up, the woman, the mom has a good job like a doctor or something.

When Moua, Toua, and their peers compare themselves to their White middle-class peers at UHS, they become painfully aware that they are poor.

Like other poor and working-class people, Americanized youth express embarrassment and shame about being poor (Fine & Weis, 1998; Willis, 1977). Toua Vang, for example, bitterly observed, "All Hmong people are poor and live in shabby houses." The shame over being poor reflects the fact that Americanized students have internalized the myth of meritocracy, which claims that all people in the United States have equal opportunities to achieve. According to this framework, merit is the only difference between the haves and have-nots. Tellingly, Toua Vang and other Americanized Hmong youth refer to low-income housing as the "ghetto," thereby calling on racialized images of poverty.

Americanized Hmong youth have concluded that money is the most important thing in the United States. As noted in chapter 1, there is evidence that adults in the larger Hmong American community have also come to define success in the United States in economic terms (Koltyk, 1998). The issue of money and the importance of money came up one day in Ms. Newton's 10th-grade European History class. Ms. Newton asked her class what people in the future would identify as being most important to late-20th-century and early-21st-century American society. White students responded that family, religion, and technology were the most important things in American society. Jim Her, a second-generation Hmong youth who struggled in school, volunteered that people in the future would identify money as being the most important thing in the United States. The conversation quickly turned to a debate over what things are truly important in American society. Tellingly, all the Hmong students agreed that, "money is the most important thing in America." Jim Her explained, "You can get most things with money." Not insignificantly, money is crucial to acquiring the symbols of Americanization.

Every Americanized youth with whom I spoke reported that they want to have more money than their parents do. In fact, many of them said they want "to be really rich." Without exception, second-generation students assert that getting an education is important because it leads to a good job. Despite their professed beliefs regarding the instrumental value of education, not all students planned to use education as the route to social mobility. Some students were more vague about their dreams of achieving wealth, and still others fantasized about striking it rich by winning the lottery. For Americanized youth, having money represents not only economic security and the ability to buy material goods, but it also represents status, power, and privilege. With money they will be able to buy the symbols of Americanization (e.g., clothes, cars, homes) that they covet and believe will bring them greater acceptance. In short, these students recognize that money whitens (Feagin, 2000; Ong, 1999).

Surviving and Resisting the Culture of Whiteness

My fieldwork confirmed Mrs. Her's observations regarding the growing number of second-generation students who are experiencing difficulties at UHS. Like other working-class and poor youth (Eckert, 1989; Willis, 1977), an increasing number of second-generation/Americanized Hmong youth are disconnected from school. Of course, there are Americanized students who are academically successful and a few who manage to make the honor roll, but the number of second-generation students who struggle academically is alarming. Although all Americanized youth spoke about the importance of school, their actions often contradicted their professed beliefs in the importance of education. Most Americanized students reported spending little time studying, and a growing number were regularly truant from school. One Americanized student who was chronically truant explained that she and her friends skip classes because they "are just tired of the teachers."

Research on other immigrant groups points to similar patterns of academic resistance among second-generation youth (Valenzuela, 1999; Zhou & Bankston, 1998). In his research on Hmong youth in Chicago, for example, Thao (1999) argued that youth who are "over-Americanized" are particularly vulnerable to gangs. Significantly, these researchers have identified youth culture and the process of Americanization as the causes of problems. My data, however, suggest students' negative attitudes toward school are partially formed in response to their experiences with an educational institution that does not serve their needs. In other words, I argue that youth cultures are influenced by negative school experiences.

Unlike traditional students, who had good relationships with their ESL teachers, few Americanized students had established good relationships with teachers or administrators. The struggle to find an advisor for the Hmong Cultural Club during the 1999–2000 academic year illustrates the distance between Americanized youth and UHS adults. As noted earlier, Ms. Bowman served as the advisor to the Hmong Cultural Club during the 1998–99 academic year. Due to scheduling conflicts, however, she found that she could not continue in that position during the 1999–2000 academic year. When Ms. Bowman encouraged the members of the Hmong Cultural Club to generate a list of potential advisors from among the UHS faculty and staff, the students were unable to come up with any names. A few students approached me about advising their club, but I explained that it might be a conflict of interest and against the school's policies. I knew from previous conversations with Americanized youth that they would not consider asking Mrs. Her to be the advisor because they viewed her as an ally of the traditional Hmong students who were "goody two-shoes." Americanized students recognized that Mrs. Her identified them as "bad kids," and they asserted they could not trust her because she would report their behavior to their parents. I also knew that they would not consider the other Hmong bilingual resource specialist because he had not made any efforts to get to know Americanized students.

At one point Ms. Bowman asked the members of the Hmong Cultural Club if they would be open to joining the Asian Club, but the students dismissed this idea as being out of the question. When I asked why they preferred the Hmong Cultural Club to the Asian Club, several girls responded, "I love the Hmong people" and "I can relate to Hmong people." They explained that they "don't have a problem with other Asians," but wanted to be with their own ethnic group. In this instance, these

Americanized students were rejecting the panethnic Asian category and asserting a specific identity as Hmong (Espiritu, 1992; Lee, 1996). Americanized students were interested in having their own space to explore and express being Hmong. As a marginalized group within the school, these students sought a safe space to discuss their experiences and simply be who they are free from the gaze of outsiders (Weis & Centrie, 2002).

Although they rejected a panethnic alliance in this case, on other occasions some of these same students expressed a panethnic consciousness, particularly with other Southeast Asians. When I asked Americanized youth what they had in common with other Southeast Asians, they pointed to cultural similarities and common experiences with racism. One Americanized male explained, "All Americans think that Asians eat cats and dogs, we don't. They think that all Asians got slanted eyes. And they think we are in gangs." Their panethnic consciousness, however, did not as readily extend to East Asian American students. Interestingly, Americanized youth described middle-class East Asian American students who socialized with Whites as being more like Whites than like Asians.

Just when it appeared that the Hmong Cultural Club might have to be suspended, Ms. Bowman was able to identify a temporary advisor for the club—a Hmong American woman hired by the school district to work with Southeast Asian parents. As the new advisor, she made efforts to educate the students about options for higher education and to help students forge networks with Hmong American students at other local high schools. Most of the regular members of the Hmong Cultural Club were largely unresponsive to information about higher education, but they were very excited about the possibility of socializing with other Hmong American youth. During the remainder of the academic year the Hmong Cultural Club organized sporting competitions with other Hmong clubs in the city.

Although many Americanized students express resistance to school, they are not entirely rejecting the idea that education can lead to economic success. They recognize that some people use education to get ahead in society, but because of their negative experiences in school they question whether education is the best way *for them* to achieve economic mobility. Many students simply assume that they are not smart enough to do well in school. Many low-achieving students have internalized their shame and think of themselves as "stupid." Jane Vue, for example, is one year behind in school because she failed her sophomore year. When she revealed this information to me she said sarcastically that it was "the Hmong way" to be at least one year behind.

Other students question whether it makes sense to put off making money now in order to earn a high school diploma. "G," for example, should be a senior in high school, but has only earned enough credits to be a sophomore. "G" explains that her part-time job is more important than school because she earns money to buy herself clothes and to travel to Hmong soccer tournaments in cities throughout the Midwest. "G" dropped out of high school in 2000 in order to work full-time. The last time I saw "G" she told me that she hopes to earn her high school equivalency degree. Her interest in obtaining a GED suggests that she has not rejected education, but has only rejected her school experience.

Some research has suggested that resistant youth of color accuse their high-achieving peers of "acting White," thereby creating a culture that is antischool (Fordham & Ogbu, 1986). Despite the growing number of Americanized youth who experienced academic difficulties and Jane's comments about "the Hmong way," I did not find any evidence that academic achievement was viewed as a White enterprise. Students like Jane and "G," for example, admire successful Hmong American youth. Americanized youth who managed to stay connected to other Hmong youth and perform well in school were particularly respected.

One day I found a group of Americanized students huddled around a cafeteria table pointing to photographs of Hmong American high school and college students in the Hmong yearbook published by the Hmong American Free Press. Unlike official school yearbooks, the Hmong yearbook included students from throughout the United States in high school through graduate school. Next to each photograph the students listed their hobbies, e-mail addresses, educational backgrounds, future goals, and hometowns. Americanized youth reported that they purchased this yearbook and not the UHS yearbook because the Hmong yearbook allowed them to make connections to other Hmong in the United States. Interestingly, Americanized youth described college graduates as having "made it." Included in the yearbook were photos of Paradise, a popular Hmong American singing group that sang hip-hop and pop songs in Hmong and English. Dressed in hip-hop–style clothes, members of Paradise listed their educational accomplishments along with their future dreams. Americanized students explained that Paradise performed at all "of the best Hmong parties."

Understanding Academic Struggles

Many of the academic difficulties that Americanized/second-generation students face are related to their continuing struggles to master academic English-language skills. Like many former ESL students, second-generation Hmong youth at UHS can speak fluent English, but struggle with reading and writing. Critics of ESL programs argue that the problems that second-language students have reading and writing are related to the fact that most ESL programs focus on oral English skills at the expense of reading and writing skills (Olsen, 1997; Valenzuela, 1999). Significantly, second-generation youth appear to have more difficulty acquiring academic English than their 1.5-generation peers. While traditional students can rely on their native-language skills to learn English, most Americanized students possess relatively weak native-language skills. It is important to note that Americanized youth at UHS are the products of years of ESL classes that have focused on helping them transition to an English-only environment. All of the Americanized students reported that they were in ESL classes in elementary school and many reported that they were in ESL classes through middle school as well. In her critique of ESL programs, Valenzuela (1999) writes:

> The very rationale of English as a Second Language (ESL)—the Predominant language program at the high school level—is subtractive. As ESL programs are designed to transition youth into an English only curriculum, they neither reinforce their native language skills nor their cultural identities. (p. 26)

As the previous discussion of Ms. Heinemann's pedagogy suggests, ESL classes do not have to be entirely subtractive. Unfortunately, most Americanized youth appear to have experienced ESL classes that were subtractive in nature. When I asked Americanized students about their experiences in ESL classes in elementary and middle school, few could recall any opportunities to learn about or share information about the Hmong culture. Like other victims of subtractive schooling, the Americanized Hmong American youth have not been allowed to develop their native-language skills. Ironically, the exclusive focus on English has made it difficult for them to acquire fluency in academic English.

Because Americanized students speak colloquial English fluently, it is often difficult for teachers to recognize the fact that many students struggle with academic language skills (*Wisconsin School News*, November 2001). Thus, students can often hide their problems until they are failing exams and their grades drop. In response to failing grades, many students simply give up and start skipping class. For example, "G" started skipping class in ninth grade because she was struggling to keep up with her classes. In my conversations with UHS teachers, they expressed confusion over why so many second-generation Hmong students continued to struggle with academic English skills. The teachers' confusion reveals a lack of understanding regarding the structure of ESL programs and the nature of language acquisition (Tse, 2001; Valdes, 2001). As noted in chapter 2, many mainstream teachers assume that Hmong American youth who struggle academically belong back in ESL. Since most Americanized youth are more comfortable speaking English than Hmong, it is clear that they do not belong in ESL programs. Furthermore, it is important to point out that Americanized youth view ESL as a stigmatized space and resist any association with the ESL program.

Americanized students interpret teachers' attempts to send students to ESL as evidence that teachers do not care about Hmong students. According to Mr. Schenk, many of the problems that Hmong students have can be traced to negative experiences with UHS educators:

> Every kid that I have talked to, whether they are sort of these hard gang members or whomever, that are Hmong, they feel like this place just doesn't fit them. If you listen to the actual words, you know, "the teacher doesn't like me," "I don't have anyplace to go," "I don't like the principals."

My fieldwork confirmed Mr. Schenk's observations that many Hmong American youth are alienated by their interactions with UHS educators.

Americanized students assumed that their teachers were racist and did not care about them. Their belief that UHS staff are uncaring was often fueled by miscommunication between the groups. When, for example, no UHS faculty or staff attended the Southeast Asian Graduation in 2000, Americanized students interpreted their absence as evidence that UHS adults don't care about Hmong students. The absence of UHS staff, however, was more than likely due to the fact that the Southeast Asian Graduation was held on the same day as the UHS prom. Nonetheless, I would argue that this scheduling conflict reveals the lack of communication between the school and the Southeast Asian American community. One semester there was a rumor that one of the vice principals had made racist comments about Hmong students. Although the Americanized students were angry about the alleged comment, most were not shocked to hear that a school authority might have made racist comments.

Unlike the traditional students, who have somewhat sheltered experiences in the ESL program, most Americanized students are in mainstream classes where they find themselves being compared to upper-middle-class White students advantaged by the school's culture of whiteness. Many middle-class White students grow up taking music lessons, attending theater camps, visiting museums, and participating in other activities valued by UHS educators. These students can trade their cultural capital for places in the school orchestra, parts in school plays, and high grades. While the experiences of White middle-class students are valued and rewarded by UHS, the experiences of Hmong American students are largely ignored.

The things that Hmong American students learn at home and in their communities are not valued by the school. In short, Hmong American students lack the cultural capital valued by UHS.

Some Americanized students reported instances of being silenced in their classes. They reported that teachers and non-Hmong students did not seem to value their opinions or experiences. They explained that teachers often "act like they want to hear what you think, but there is only one right answer." In some cases, the "one right answer" represents a particular political bias. As Fine (1991) writes, "Silencing is about who can speak, what can and cannot be spoken and whose discourse must be controlled" (p. 33). The following excerpt from my field notes provides an example of one student's experience of being silenced in a class:

> Sia was very upset today about what happened in her social studies
> class. Apparently, the teacher had asked students to debate the
> issue of low-income housing. Sia said that she was the only person
> in the class to support low-income housing and that she felt all
> alone in her efforts to talk about why it is good to have low-income
> housing. She said that most of the students in her class are White.
> She complained bitterly that many of the students in the class said
> "stupid things about how people shouldn't just get stuff for free." I
> asked Sia whether the teacher tried to balance the debate by giving
> the other side and she said, "No! She just stood there and smiled." I
> wish I had been in class.

As a student who has lived in low-income housing, this debate was not simply academic for Sia. She understood that the students and teacher were passing judgment on people like her. This class once again confirmed for her that she was not valued at the school.

Many Americanized students have responded to their position at UHS by maintaining their distance from teachers and other members of the professional staff. During her senior year in high school, Sia was having serious family problems that led her to miss many days of school. Near the end of her senior year she was in jeopardy of flunking out of school. When I suggested that she tell her teachers or counselors about her problems, she refused because she didn't trust them to treat her with respect. Sia argued that her teachers did not really know her or want to know her. Sia maintained that her teachers would not understand that she had to miss school in order to take care of her younger brothers. In short, she was convinced that teachers at UHS don't care about students like her. Because trust is crucial to student and teacher relationships, the loss of trust impedes the educational process (Erickson, 1987). In the absence of trusting relationships with their teachers, it is not surprising that many second-generation students feel isolated and unsupported at UHS.

Not insignificantly, those Americanized students who had the most positive relationships with UHS faculty and administrators were those who dressed and carried themselves like White students. Unlike the majority of Americanized students, these students did not wear the baggy pants associated with urban youth, and appeared to be avoiding the stigma associated with wearing hip-hop–style clothing. As one of these more successful Americanized student said, "I don't dress ghetto. I dress more regular, normal." These successful Americanized students avoided the use of hip-hop language, which teachers associated with African American students.

It is important to note that even the more academically successful Americanized youth are negatively affected by the culture of whiteness at UHS. Academically successful students expressed anxiety about competing against White middle-class students. For example, as mentioned in chapter 2, Pang appreciates his parents' support to succeed in school but recognizes that they can't help him in the ways that "American" parents can. Although Pang did graduate from UHS and go on to attend technical college in the fall of 1999, he never saw himself as a success. Pang's attitude toward his achievements was shared by other academically successful Americanized youth.

Moua Y, mentioned earlier in this chapter, is another example of a successful second-generation student. Moua graduated from UHS in 2000 with a B average and planned to go to technical college to earn her associate degree before going on to pursue her bachelor's degree. Although Moua was always able to keep up in her classes, she rarely spoke in her classes because she didn't think she had anything important or interesting to say. While Pang and Moua recognized that White middle-class students were privileged by their parents' educational backgrounds, the culture of whiteness at UHS did not encourage them to develop the tools to criticize that privilege. In the absence of a critical framework, Pang and Moua assumed that their White middle-class peers were simply smarter than they are. The Internalization of White superiority served to silence them in classes, and their silence limited their success in classes that valued classroom participation.

Calls for Culturally Relevant Pedagogy and "Teachers Who Care"

As I have already argued, many Americanized students have concluded that teachers don't care about them. These students long for teachers who care about them as people and who demonstrate respect for Hmong culture. Students who struggle with chronic truancy are among the ones with the most well-defined definitions of good teachers. Sia, for example, had clear ideas about how teachers should treat their students. She asserted "good teachers know you and care about you." Sia claims that "good teachers" should know about the lives of students inside and outside of school. As noted earlier, Sia was convinced that her teachers did not care about her. Similarly, Toua Lee, a senior in the class of 1999, explained that she appreciates educators who listen to her problems and concerns without passing judgment on her or the Hmong culture. According to Sia and Toua, "good teachers" demonstrate that they truly care about their students' lives. Similarly, Valenzuela (1999) found that Mexican American students "are committed to an authentic form of caring that emphasizes relations of reciprocity between teachers and students" (p. 61).

Interestingly, many adults at UHS who expressed the kind of caring that Hmong American students valued were not teachers but paraprofessionals. It is also worth noting that all of the paraprofessionals who were viewed in a positive light were African Americans. Ms. Bowman, for example, was one adult named by Americanized youth as being trustworthy. Interestingly, several Americanized youth who were chronic truants identified members of the security staff as adults they could trust. These adults were often the very ones who caught them breaking school rules and turned them in to the principals for discipline. Several students named Betty, an African American woman who worked as a security guard at UHS, as a trusted adult. On several occasions I observed Betty yelling at Hmong American students who were truant. In addition to these interactions, however, I noticed that Betty often asked students about their siblings, parents, and cousins. Betty was included in the Hmong Cultural Club photograph that appeared in the 1998–99 yearbook. "G" explained that she liked Betty and other members of the security staff because they "listen and talk and give advice about their lives."

The one teacher who was consistently described by Americanized youth as being "a good teacher" was Ms. Newton. Ms. Newton, a White woman, teaches 10th-grade European history and the Academic Skills class. A few of the Americanized youth have taken both of Ms. Newton's classes. Kate, a second-generation Hmong student in Ms. Newton's European history class, explained that she likes Ms. Newton "because she is fair. She isn't prejudiced against Hmong students." Not insignificantly, Ms. Newton stays after school on a regular basis to tutor students who are struggling academically. Ms. Newton reminds students who have been absent that she expects to meet with them to talk about what they have missed. One Americanized Hmong student who is a mother of a toddler explained that Ms. Newton has always understood when Hmong students have to miss school for family reasons. In my conversations with Ms. Newton, I was consistently struck by how much she knew about each of her students. She knew which students had been struggling academically, she knew about their family lives, and she knew about their learning styles and personalities. In short, she was interested in knowing the whole student.

Americanized Hmong youth routinely complained that they could not relate to the curriculum. They argued that UHS should offer classes on Hmong culture and history. Hope, a chronic truant who failed ninth grade, said that she would welcome a class in Hmong culture, history, or language so she could learn about "her people." When she was in elementary school, she took Hmong-language classes at the community center and still uses some of that Hmong when she participates in Hmong chat rooms. Another chronic truant, "G," read the nonfiction book *When the Spirit Catches You* by Fadimann in her Multicultural Literature class. She explained that she "loved" the book because it showed the Hmong people's perspective. Specifically, "G" appreciated that the book showed the "Americans being racist." "G" understood racism to be a part of her everyday life, and she resented the fact that the school rarely acknowledged the existence of racism. The fact that Hope and "G," both chronic truants, responded to material that focused on Hmong American culture and experiences suggests that a culturally relevant curriculum might help reconnect them to school (Ladson-Billings, 1995). In addition to curricula on Hmong culture and Hmong history, the story about Sia's experience in the debate over low-income housing suggests that a truly culturally relevant curriculum and pedagogy would provide low-income Hmong students with an opportunity to discuss issues related to social class.

Many Americanized students fail to see how academic subjects will help them get work. They questioned whether classes like algebra, Shakespeare, or chemistry will be useful in their adult lives. Tom Vue, a senior in the class of 1999, asserted that UHS should offer more vocational courses to help students learn about different jobs. Although this may sound like a straightforward plea for vocational education, Tom assumed that vocational education would help him "plan for college." Tom did not understand that courses like algebra and chemistry are required for admission to most four-year colleges. He assumed that high school business courses would be highly valued by four-year colleges and universities. Like many Americanized Hmong youth I encountered, Tom lacked the necessary information to make informed decisions about his education at UHS and beyond. Hmong American students do not belong to the social networks that can help them navigate schools (Stanton-Salazar, 2001).

Hmong American youth need to be taught explicitly about the qualifications needed for different jobs and the qualifications needed for admission to different types of postsecondary institutions. Although students of color, including Hmong Americans, have some opportunities to learn about postsecondary options, these efforts are typically sporadic. That some Americanized youth in the Hmong Cultural Club appeared uninterested in information about higher education suggests that they had lowered aspirations for their futures. I would argue that Hmong American youth need consistent and early exposure to information about postsecondary education and career options. They need to be taught the rules of the culture of power so that they can survive within that culture (Delpit, 1988).

"They Look at Us as Some Bad Kids"

In addition to conflict with school, many Americanized students experience intergenerational conflict at home. Many students routinely complained that their parents are too strict and don't understand life in the United States. While many immigrant parents only speak Hmong, most second-generation youth are more fluent in English. Like traditional students, most Americanized students are expected to perform caring work and household chores. For Americanized youth, however, these role reversals often lead to the weakening of parental authority. Having to help their parents do routine activities confirms for many second-generation youth that their parents are somehow deficient. Portes and Rumbaut (1996) assert that the loss of parental authority is directly related to the fact that the parental generation has not acculturated at the same rate as their children.

> Generational dissonance occurs when second generation acculturation is neither guided nor accompanied by changes in the first generation. This situation leads directly to role reversal in those instances when first-generation parents lack sufficient education or sufficient integration into the ethnic community to cope with the outside environment and hence must depend on their children's guidance. (p. 241)

Another source of tension between Americanized youth and their parents involves the way teens dress. For Hmong parents, the baggy clothes worn by their American-born children are signs of gang membership. Hope complained:

> They look at us as some bad kids. They call us some little
> gangbangers. 'Cause the people around us, the way we dress and
> stuff. Mostly they don't, they don't—people started dressing all
> baggy and they don't like it. People, like the old folks, they just say

that we've forgotten our language a little bit, we have a little bit.
But then, we still carry our traditions and stuff around.

She understands that her clothes make her "look like a thug" in her parents' eyes, but she maintains that she and her friends are not in gangs. Because of their clothing, however, Hmong elders and many school authorities assume that she and her friends are involved with gangs and treat them with suspicion. Not insignificantly, school authorities influence Hmong parents' attitudes toward the hip-hop clothing worn by Americanized youth. At a gang prevention workshop for Southeast Asian parents, school district staff informed parents that baggy pants were among the first signs of gang involvement. Criticized by adults, many Americanized students like Hope cling more tightly to an oppositional identity for a sense of belonging. This oppositional identity, however, further alienates them from school and the Hmong adult community.

Hope's words also point to the breakdown in communication between generations when youth lose their native language. Hope explains that she would like to learn more about her culture and history, but her level of Hmong fluency makes it difficult to talk about complicated subjects with her parents. The fact that Hope and many of her Americanized peers struggle to communicate in Hmong is evidence that their schooling has successfully subtracted away aspects of their language and culture (Tse, 2001; Valenzuela, 1999).

Immigrant parents view the changing family roles, their children's desire for increased independence, and their children's clothes as evidence that they are losing their second-generation children to "American ways." Some immigrant parents have responded to the situation by trying to further control all aspects of their children's lives. Similarly, Suarez-Orozco and Suarez-Orozco (2001) discovered that Latino immigrant parents may "over-restrict the activities of the children and attempt to minimize the host country's influence" (p. 65). Americanized Hmong youth respond to their parents' hypercontrol by resisting parental authority. Resistance may come in the form of direct confrontation or in the form of indirect challenges to parental authority behind their backs. Toua Vang has had problems with truancy for the past 2 years. She explains that she skips class because "school is the only time we can hang out with our friends." When she isn't in school, Toua Vang and her friends are expected to be at home helping with chores, but at school she and her friends have figured out that they control their own time. Thus, truancy is a way to get around their parents' control.

Toua Vang and Hope are examples of students who experience significant conflict with their parents. As pointed out earlier, this intergenerational conflict is related to differences in acculturation. According to Portes and

Rumbaut (2001), dissonant acculturation occurs "when children's learning of the English language and American ways and simultaneous loss of
the immigrant culture outstrip their parents'" (p. 54). Americanized students like Toua and Hope are the ones most likely to complain that their
parents are "too traditional."

In other cases, however, when acculturation is more or less conso-
nant between the generations, the intergenerational conflict is less severe
(Portes & Rumbaut, 1996, 2001). Moua, for example, described her relationship with her parents as being "pretty good." She explained that her
parents are "traditional, but not real traditional" and they are "strict, but
not superstrict." Moua explained that her parents allow her and her siblings to pick their own clothes even though they do not really approve of
the trendy urban styles clothes that she and her siblings wear. Moua also
points out that her parents have emphasized the importance of education
for girls and boys. In contrast to many Hmong parents who insist that their
daughters remain close to home until marriage, Moua's parents have even
allowed their oldest daughter to go to college in California. Although her
parents have made accommodations to life in the United States, they still
emphasize the importance of family. Like daughters in many Hmong families, Moua is expected to help with the cooking, cleaning, and care of
younger siblings. Moua's older brother plans to help his parents out financially when he finishes school. The fact that Moua's parents have been
willing to make compromises has helped to limit the intergenerational
conflict within the family and helped to maintain parental authority. In
short, Moua's parents' strategy of accommodation without assimilation
(Gibson, 1988), or selective acculturation (Portes & Rumbaut, 2001), helps
to keep intergenerational difficulties from exploding.

Interpreting Americanized Teens

Americanized youths' understandings of what it means to be Hmong in
the United States are informed by their relationships with their parents,
and their marginalized positions in school and the larger society. Many
Americanized youth have embraced an oppositional identity, as symbol-
ized by their hip-hop style. Misunderstood as "gang" kids by parents and
teachers, Americanized youth often become further alienated from the
authority of Hmong and White adults. Americanized youths' hip-hop style
is, in part, an expression of resistance to White authority, racism, and
parental authority, but it is not in and of itself a sign of gang involvement.

Although these youths proudly assert their Americanized identities,
they also express a strong sense of ethnic solidarity. As pointed out earlier, most Americanized youth have chosen to keep their Hmong names

instead of taking on European American names. In a previous study, I found that Asian immigrant students regularly changed their names in order to fit into the culture of the school, but Americanized Hmong students at UHS held on proudly to their given names (Lee, 1996). Americanized Hmong students are quick to claim a distinct Hmong identity. In fact, their experiences at school and in the larger society confirm for them that they are Hmong. For the Americanized Hmong youth, however, their Hmong identity is different from their parents' Hmong identity and the traditional students' Hmong identity. The Hmong American singing group B4 captures the struggle of young Hmong Americans to maintain a proud Hmong identity in the United States in their song "We are H.M.O.N.G." They begin the rap song with a call to all Hmong:

> This song is a special dedication to all the Hmong people out there. No matter where you are or what you do always be proud of who you are. Don't ever let anybody tell you that you can't achieve your dreams or goals. Always keep your head up high and stand strong 'cause you are Hmong.

The song's refrain is simply, "We are H.M.O.N.G." At one point in the song there is a reference to the pain, suffering, and loss in the Hmong community and the importance of trying to achieve your dreams.

Like the members of B4, the Americanized Hmong youth at UHS are negotiating new Hmong identities in the United States. Although they experience intergenerational conflict with parents whom they describe as being "too traditional," they are not rejecting their Hmong identities or cultures. Americanized students are trying to re-create a Hmong identity in response to their experiences in the United States. Like other Asian Americans, Americanized Hmong youth are re-creating identities and cultures that are "partly inherited, partly modified, as well as partly invented"(Lowe, 1996, p. 65). Like other people of color, they are re-creating identities and cultures under unequal relations of power. Americanized youth recognize that as Hmong people they are seen as racialized other, and they have responded to the racial exclusion by adopting and identifying with the existing hip-hop culture, a culture they perceive to have oppositional power. Thus, their identities can be read as a critique of racial inequality at the school and in the larger U.S. society. Although they have adopted hip-hop styles, they are not engaging in simple imitation, but are also doing things to transform hip-hop to reflect the specific experiences of Hmong in the United States. Thus, singing groups like B4 perform in English and Hmong, and they sing about the struggles of being new to the United States.

CONCLUSION

The stories of traditional and Americanized Hmong youth serve to reinforce the reality that the process of identity construction is complex. Both
traditional and Americanized students are negotiating identities in response
to messages from home, school, and the larger society. Both groups are
forming their identities in response to messages about race. Traditional
students responded to the messages about race by emphasizing the dis-
tinctiveness of Hmong culture. These students embraced the language of
"tradition" and emphasized the aspects of the Hmong culture that are
valued by the dominant society. Traditional students did not mind being
viewed as "foreigners." As ESL students, traditional students were surrounded by other relative newcomers to the United States and generally
did not experience "foreignness" to be a negative thing. Despite the label,
traditional students do not represent untouched tradition. Like many
Hmong American leaders, traditional students attempted to highlight the
accomplishments in the Hmong community. By presenting a model minority identity they hoped to gain acceptance in the larger society. While
the Hmong American community has accomplished much and should be
proud of their successes, it is important to point out that they are forming
their identities in response to unequal relations of power.

Americanized students responded to the messages about race by attempting to distance themselves from their traditional peers and all other
things they assumed might make them appear foreign. Americanized students have adopted a hip-hop style as a form of oppositional power. They
have not "lost" their cultures or identities, but are searching for new ways
of being Hmong. For both traditional and Americanized youth, "tradition"
is something largely imagined. Similarly, both groups are negotiating what
"Americanization," "being American," and "America" mean. Chapter 4 will
focus on the way gender further complicates the construction of identity
among both traditional and Americanized Hmong students.

4

Wimps, Gangsters, Victims, and Teen Moms: The Gendered Experiences of Hmong American Youth

The Hmong culture believes that women are supposed to be this and that. I don't believe in that. If you're the woman, you have to do all this stuff. It's like giving you a job. And you don't even want to do it. It's like already setting your life for you.

Jean, Americanized girl

Both the guys and the girls have to do things. The guys do the outside work, and the girls do the inside work. Like, the guys have to take out the trash.

Danny, Americanized boy

For immigrants, the process of incorporation into U.S. society is racialized and classed, as I have argued in previous chapters. The immigrant experience, however, is also gendered. Gender, as it intersects with race and class, informs and limits the experiences of Hmong American youth in their homes, communities, schools, and the larger society. In short, what it means to be a Hmong man in the United States is, in significant ways, distinct from what it means to be a Hmong woman. Hmong American youth receive multiple and often contradictory messages about gender from their families, the Hmong community, their peers, the school, mainstream society, and popular culture. This chapter explores the gendered messages surrounding Hmong American youth and focuses on the various ways that young Hmong American men and women are understanding, constructing, and performing their gendered identities in response to these messages. The various masculinities and femininities produced by Hmong American youth converge with and complicate the traditional and Americanized categories of Hmong students discussed in the previous chapters.

DOMINANT MESSAGES ABOUT GENDER

Although there are a variety of masculinities and femininities expressed in the United States, not all expressions of gender are equal. Within the context of the dominant society, there is a single hegemonic masculinity and an ideal or emphasized femininity against which men and women are measured. As Kimmel (2000) explains, "American men and women must also contend with a dominant definition, a culturally preferred version that is held up as the model against which we are expected to measure ourselves" (p. 4). In the United States it is impossible to fully appreciate the meaning and significance of gender without recognizing the way that gender intersects with race and class (Guinier & Torres, 2002).

In discussing the historical relationship between whiteness and hegemonic masculinity, cultural anthropologist A. Ong (1999) writes, "White masculinity established qualities of manliness and civilization itself" (p. 266). Similarly, Feagin (2000) argues, "White men have been the standard for male handsomeness, as well as masculinity and manly virtue" (p. 113). Correspondingly, the very definition of a woman has been tied to whiteness (Espiritu, 2000; Guinier & Torres, 2002; R. Lee, 1999). In the mid-19th century White middle-class women were constructed as moral and chaste, thereby representing True Womanhood (R. Lee, 1999). While White middle-class women were seen as being pure, women of color were characterized as immoral (Espiritu, 2000). Thus, the identity of White middle-class women was constructed in opposition to the identities of women of color. Citing the work of historian Peggy Pascoe (1990), Robert Lee (1999) explains that the moral authority and superiority of White middle-class women during the 19th century was linked to their ability "to speak for the needs of women of other races and classes" (p. 85). In this way, White women were seen as saviors of women of color.

The centrality of whiteness to hegemonic masculinity and ideal femininity continues to persist today. Although whiteness is primary to dominant masculinity, not just any White male meets the standards set by hegemonic masculinity (Lei, 2001). The hegemonic man must also be heterosexual, able-bodied, physically fit, tall (5'10"–6'2"), independent, Christian, and economically successful. The definition of hegemonic masculinity is also constructed in opposition to definitions of femininity (i.e., men are understood to be unlike women). Furthermore, hegemonic masculinity is constructed as safe (i.e., man the protector of his wife and children). According to dominant perspectives on masculinity, men who express subordinated masculinities may have to rely on overt forms of aggression to maintain authority, but men who possess hegemonic masculinities do not have to rely on physical power for their authority (Connell, 1995). Boys/men who do not express the behaviors and traits associated with hegemonic masculinity within a given community are identified as possessing deficient masculinities that are subordinate to the hegemonic masculinity.

Like the hegemonic male in U.S. society, the ideal female is White, middle-class, able bodied, Christian, and heterosexual. The woman who possesses ideal or emphasized femininity, however, is in other ways very different from the hegemonic man (Connell, 1995). While the hegemonic male must be economically self-sufficient, the ideal female may be dependent on her husband. In fact, a woman's status is ultimately tied to her relationship with a male partner (Holland & Eisenhart, 1991). The ideal woman must conform to a physical type in order to attract a man, and whiteness is central to the ideal of female beauty (Collins, 2000). Messages about the ideal woman dominate popular and consumer culture. Gillespie (1998) notes that women who are represented as beautiful in popular and consumer cultures conform to a White body aesthetic (e.g., blonde, blue-eyed, thin, long hair, voluptuous). Not insignificantly, women of color who are held up as icons of beauty often conform in some ways to White standards of beauty.

IDEAL MASCULINITIES AND FEMININITIES AT UHS

As in the dominant society, whiteness is central to hegemonic masculinity at UHS. Although young men of all races can gain status for athletic achievements, the most honored status at the school goes to White males who are academically successful (i.e., college-bound) and involved in one or more high status extracurricular activities (e.g., sports, music, student government). The star athlete on the football or basketball team certainly achieves status at UHS, but unless he is also a good student he falls short of hegemonic masculinity. It is worth noting that academic achievement is central to the definition of hegemonic masculinity because education is valued by the highly educated community in which UHS is located. Significantly, higher education is required for the kind of white-collar jobs that middle-class White parents expect their sons to have when they grow up. Thus, the hegemonic male at UHS is White, plays on a varsity sports team or is involved with another high status activity, and does well academically.

Similar to hegemonic males at other schools, young men who embody hegemonic masculinity at UHS express their gendered power by taking up space, both literally and figuratively, in classrooms and corridors and on playing fields (Orenstein, 1994; Thorne, 1993). These young men garner athletic awards, are elected to the prom court, and are chosen as graduation speakers. Like the pro-school "jocks" in Eckert's (1989) classic study, the hegemonic male at UHS has the run of the school. They enjoy friendly relationships with teachers and administrators, and are described as "all-American boys." Not insignificantly, White males are the only ones honored with this title. Thus, hegemonic masculinity at UHS, like hegemonic masculinity in the larger society, is linked to race, personality, and individual achievement (Kimmel, 1994; Kumashiro, 1998).

Like the hegemonic male at UHS, the ideal UHS girl is White. She is also academically successful, involved in extracurricular activities, and college-bound. Furthermore, she is socially popular with other girls and with boys. She dresses in the latest clothes from the Gap and Abercrombie that mark her middle-class whiteness (Greenhouse, 2003; Perry, 2001). She is the type of student to be recognized in the senior poll for her beauty or her friendliness. She might play on a school athletic team, but she would also be on the prom court. Finally, she gets along well with teachers and administrators, who see her as being smart, trustworthy, and sweet.

There were a few East Asian American and South Asian American girls at UHS who appeared to have achieved a high social status within the mainstream of the school. Although I did not interview any of these students, teachers identified them as examples of successful Asian American students. All of these Asian American young women were involved in high-status extracurricular activities, performed well academically, and socialized with White students. I also noticed that they tended to dress in styles similar to the mainstream White students at the school. Interestingly, teachers and Hmong and non-Hmong students referred to these East Asian American and South Asian American females as being "Americanized." Here, the term *Americanized* seems to be a stand in for "whitened." I am not arguing that they were whitewashed but that they were read as acting like White people. As I listened to the Hmong students talk about these Americanized Asian Americans, I was once again reminded that they might view my own behavior as being White.

WIMPS, GANGSTERS, VICTIMS, AND TEEN MOMS: PERCEPTIONS OF HMONG YOUTH

Conversations with UHS educators and non-Hmong students revealed that Hmong American males are viewed as lacking the qualities associated with hegemonic masculinity. Teachers remarked that Hmong males were quieter in class than other males and were not involved in school activities. Some teachers concluded that the boys were quiet because of language or other cultural issues. Because quietness is associated with femininity, Asian American men have often been constructed as effeminate and therefore not masculine. Cheung (1993) notes, "Precisely because quietness is associated with the feminine, as is the 'East' in relation to the 'West' (in Orientalist discourse), Asian and Asian American men too have been 'feminized' in American popular culture" (p. 2). The characterization of Asian and Asian American men as feminine renders them harmless in the eyes of the dominant culture. Seen as too quiet, passive, nerdy, and small, Asian American men fail to exhibit the form of masculinity valued by the dominant American society (Kumashiro, 1998; R. Lee, 1999; Lei, 2001, 2003). Asian American men are thus easily dismissed as inconsequential. At UHS, teachers who assumed that Hmong American boys are quiet because of language and other cultural differences simply ignored them. Although these teachers perceived Hmong American males as being *culturally different and foreign*, they noted that they had never had any problems with them in class.

There were other moments, however, when the dominant group viewed the quietness of Asian American men as potentially dangerous and threatening. A few teachers, for example, expressed fears that some Hmong American boys were hiding their gang involvement behind their quiet demeanors. It is worth mentioning that Hmong American boys who dressed in clothes associated with urban youth were the ones suspected of being involved with gangs. Thus, Hmong American boys who wore hip-hop–style clothing were blackened in the eyes of White teachers. One teacher asserted that gang involvement was prevalent among young Hmong men.

> I get the feeling that there are, that there are a lot of kids [Hmong males and other males of color] who are involved in gangs. And often, it will be, kids will be involved, and then it's just a part of life. You know, it's not even a question, of course you're involved in a gang for protection.

White boys, according to this teacher, were rarely in gangs. Although this teacher was convinced that many Hmong boys were involved in gangs, the teacher admitted to not really knowing many Hmong boys at the school. Like other UHS educators, it appeared that this teacher defined any group of male students of color who dressed in hip-hop clothing as likely gang members. This teacher and others who feared that Hmong American boys were involved with gangs believed that school officials should keep a watch on the boys. The image that Hmong males are at risk for gang involvement is linked to perceptions that Hmong youth are *culturally deprived*. The stereotype of the Hmong gang member appears to be widespread in the Midwest. For example, preservice teachers at a university in the Midwest pointed to gang involvement as one of the few things they had heard about the Hmong community (Hobbel, 2003). In her study of race relations at a multiracial high school, Lei (2001) found that the quietness of Southeast Asian American males was constructed as both "understandable" because they were culturally different and "unsettling" because they might be gang members.

The stereotype of the mysterious Asian American gang member represents the dominant group's fears about Asian American masculinity. The Asian or Asian American gang member represents the alien threat living among "real" Americans (R. Lee, 1999). Asian American gang members and those assumed to belong to gangs are understood to be dangerous and threatening to American society. They express a masculinity that at first glance may appear to be similar to the hypermasculinity associated with African American boys and men (Kumashiro, 1998; Lei, 2001). Ferguson (2000) argues that schools perceive the expression of African American masculinity as being of "an inherent vicious, insubordinate nature that as a threat to order must be controlled" (p. 86). Like the hypermasculinity associated with African American boys/men, the Asian gang member is represented as being a problem that needs to be monitored. The difference between the hypermasculinity associated with African Americans and the hypermasculinity of Asian gang members surrounds the construction of each group's sexuality. While African American boys/men are hypersexualized, the Asian American gangbangers are represented as being sexually ambiguous, feminine, or asexual (R. Lee, 1999). Thus, the characterizations of Hmong American males at UHS as either quiet (i.e., harmless) or quiet (i.e., dangerous) mirrors stereotypes of Asian American men in general. In either case, Hmong American males are implicitly understood to lack hegemonic masculinity.

While most UHS faculty and staff either ignored Hmong American boys or viewed them with suspicion, they were more likely to view Hmong American girls in a relatively positive light. Hmong girls were more likely than Hmong boys to have friendly contact with non-Hmong students and staff. While Hmong American boys were seen as lacking most of the qualities associated with legitimate masculinity, Hmong American girls were seen as possessing some qualities consistent with dominant ideas about femininity. For example, many teachers described Hmong girls as being quiet, but teachers did not seem to view quietness among girls to be suspicious. This may be related to dominant ideas regarding gender, which dictate that girls and women shouldn't be too loud. The majority of Hmong females also fit into dominant ideas about ideal body size for girls/women (read: small and thin). Like other Asian American women, Hmong American young women are viewed as hyperfeminine (Espiritu, 2000).

The staff's ideas about the subordinate position of women in Hmong culture also made Hmong female students sympathetic characters. The practice of early marriage was most often cited as an example of the oppressive sexism of Hmong culture. Here, Hmong females are seen as victims in need of being saved. Significantly, the practices of early marriage and early childbearing were often the only things that male and female members of the UHS staff knew about the Hmong culture. In my own classes at the University of Wisconsin I have been struck by the fact that the Hmong practice of early marriage is the first thing that my White undergraduates will talk about when I mention that I've been doing research on the Hmong American community.

In comparing the position of boys and girls within Hmong families, one teacher asserted, "I think the girls have to grow up faster in terms of taking on home responsibilities. I think the workload is inequitable outside of school. And then this whole issue of, you know, who gets to decide when you marry, who you marry . . ." White female members of the staff consistently expressed concern regarding the impact of Hmong gender expectations on the education of Hmong girls. Mrs. Quigley, the school nurse, observed that Hmong females must juggle their roles as wives and mothers in addition to being students.

> And oftentimes they truly have at least three jobs. One is as students and they're almost always committed to education . . . Then they are the wife, and sometimes they are subservient to their husbands and really do take on much more of the parenting role, girls are the parents, and then there is the housework.

The nurse went on to compare the maturity of Hmong mothers with the immaturity/lack of responsibility of other teen mothers.

Although most of the White members of the UHS staff viewed the practice of early marriage as being problematic, they responded to Hmong girls in a variety of ways. Many teachers mentioned their concern about early marriage among Hmong females, but appeared to have little personal contact with Hmong girls. These teachers tended to hold rather static and essentialized images of Hmong culture and fit into the group of UHS teachers who described Hmong students as being *culturally different*. A few educators viewed the practice of early marriage as a threat to the larger society that must be contained. These educators used the language of *cultural deprivation* to describe Hmong American students. Finally, a few educators spoke about the importance of educating, helping, and empowering young Hmong women. Like the first group of educators, these adults believed that Hmong girls were victims of a patriarchal culture.

White women on the UHS staff were particularly concerned about gender norms within the Hmong community and were the most likely to be involved in efforts to help Hmong girls. Those who worked closely with ESL students commonly forged relationships with Hmong female students. These women assumed that it was their responsibility to help newcomers, including Hmong girls, fit into the mainstream of society. They viewed Hmong cultural expectations regarding gender to be the biggest barrier faced by Hmong females attempting to get an education. Rather than simply imposing their perspectives on gender, however, these women tried to understand the young women's situations. Mrs. Quigley, for example, was clear that she did not want to judge the Hmong culture, but wanted to provide Hmong female students with information to make their own choices regarding their lives. In previous years Ms. Stockton, one of the school social workers, organized support groups for Hmong mothers that encouraged the young women to share information with each other. Ms. Stockton's descriptions of these support groups suggest that young Hmong women need "safe spaces" to discuss their fears, hopes, and insecurities (Weis & Centrie, 2002).

These White female educators believed that education is the route to economic and social independence for all women, and they communicated this to Hmong American girls. From this perspective, education is key to successfully resisting gender inequality. In her ethnographic study of Dominican, West Indian, and Haitian youth, Lopez (2003) discovered that female teachers were inclined to favor girls over boys. Lopez (2003) argues that schools are institutions saturated with feminist ideologies that support girls. She writes:

> Against the backdrop of demands for racial, gender and sexual preference equality, a critical mass of women teachers have imparted a gender identity that is inextricably linked to feminist practices, namely pursuing an education as a means of achieving independence. (p. 110)

Like Lopez, I would argue that many White female teachers see education as the route to gender equality; however, I would emphasize that White women often view gender along cultural lines. Specifically, the White women in my study appeared to focus on the sexism that Hmong American girls face within the Hmong culture, viewing them as being more oppressed than other groups of girls at the school. Although I agree that gender norms in the Hmong community are more rigid and hierarchical than mainstream American gender norms, I would also argue that it is important not to ignore the gender inequalities in mainstream society. Furthermore, while these White women went to great efforts to assist young Hmong women, they failed to fully appreciate the role that racism played in the daily lives of Hmong students of both genders.

Ms. Nelson, a guidance counselor, was among the UHS educators who viewed the Hmong practice of early marriage as a problem for the larger society. She expressed concern that early marriage compromises the education of Hmong American youth and prevents the Hmong community from becoming economically self-sufficient. In response to her questions regarding how UHS could support Hmong female students, I suggested that the school invite a diverse group of Hmong women (e.g., unmarried college women, married women with children, divorced women) to speak to the Hmong girls. Ms. Nelson asserted that she would be more than happy to bring in Hmong American college women who had postponed marriage, but she did not want to include any women who had married and had children as teens. She reasoned that bringing in young mothers might encourage girls to get married, and she asserted that she wants to push postponing marriage. Ms. Nelson seemed to assume that all married women would automatically encourage early marriage. Her approach would mean the silencing of the complexity of the young women's experiences and concerns.

Ms. Nelson's attitudes about early marriage are linked to her concerns about poverty in the Hmong community. She fears that early marriage will lead to a cycle of poverty for the Hmong community. Similarly, Mrs. Barnard, an English teacher, remarked that Hmong youth are "at risk," and that early marriage is turning the Hmong into the "new underclass." From this perspective, early marriage is a problem not only for Hmong women and the Hmong community, but for the larger American society as well. Furthermore, it is important to recognize that descriptions such as "at risk" and "underclass" are racialized terms associated with African Americans (Lipman, 1998). Thus, early marriage and early childbearing become blackened in the dominant rhetoric.

MESSAGES ABOUT GENDER FROM THE HMONG AMERICAN COMMUNITY

The Hmong culture is most often characterized in the academic literature as being highly patriarchal, with rigid gender roles for men and women (Donnelly, 1994; Faderman & Xiong, 1998). In Laos, men were responsible for the economic well-being of their families and for making all decisions regarding the family's welfare. Women were responsible for bearing and raising many children. Additionally, women performed the cooking and cleaning and helped with the farm labor. The patrilineal and patriarchal clan system shaped gender relations between husbands and wives and between parents and children (Donnelly, 1994; Faderman & Xiong, 1998). Men were the undisputed leaders in families. Women were to walk behind their husbands, and were allowed to eat only after the men in the family had eaten (Faderman & Xiong, 1998). Men could engage in polygamous relationships, but women could not. Although children were taught to listen to their mother, the father's word was understood to represent the final authority.

Male children were particularly prized because they carried on the family name. As adults, male children became responsible for the care of their parents. Although valued, female children were viewed as temporary members of the family since they became members of their husband's family upon marriage. As in many rural societies, Hmong girls were encouraged to marry during early adolescence. Tellingly, the men in the family arranged the marriage contracts (Donnelly, 1994; Faderman & Xiong, 1998).

Early research on Hmong refugee students in the United States discovered that Hmong girls, in particular, experienced serious problems in school, including high dropout rates from middle and high school (Cohn, 1986; Goldstein, 1985). Researchers concluded that the emphasis on early marriage and motherhood within in the Hmong community led to high dropout rates among girls (Donnelly, 1994; Goldstein, 1985; Rumbaut & Ima, 1988). In discussing the high dropout rates among Hmong girls, Rumbaut and Ima (1988) pointed to the "patrilineal and patriarchal norms that tend to devalue females among the Hmong" (p. xiv).

While the Hmong refugee community was initially ambivalent about the education of girls, they immediately embraced education for boys and young men (Rumbaut & Ima, 1988). The Hmong American community supported education for boys because sons were seen as being responsible for supporting their parents in their old age. Thus, the education of sons was seen as an investment for the family. During this period education became a new way for Hmong boys and men to gain status in the United States, but Hmong girls continued to gain status only through early marriage and motherhood, as they had in Laos (Donnelly,1994; Goldstein, 1985).

Gender roles and norms have continued to shift over the last 25 years as Hmong men and women create and re-create gender roles in response to social, economic, and political conditions in the United States. While men continue to be viewed as community and family leaders, particularly among the older generation (Hein, 1996), women are beginning to make their voices heard within the Hmong American community. For example, at a meeting between the Lakeview mayor and leaders of the Southeast Asian American community, there were several men and one Hmong woman present. The first Hmong American to be elected to the Minnesota state legislature is a woman. Younger women have been particularly successful in gaining positions of authority within Hmong American organizations formed by U.S. educated Hmong. For example, they have been the primary organizers of recent national conferences directed at young Hmong Americans (Lee, 1997).

Economic forces in the United States have had a particularly profound impact on gender relations within Hmong families. Hmong parents now view education for their sons and daughters as necessary for economic security. Many women who interrupted their studies to marry as teens are returning to school in order to get better jobs (Fass, 1991; Lee, 1997). Economic forces have also led some younger Hmong women to want smaller families (Faderman & Xiong, 1998; Lee, 1997). Parents now hold varied ideas regarding when their daughters should marry. Increasingly, some parents encourage the postponement of marriage until after high school. Others encourage marriage during high school, but still emphasize the importance of graduating from high school. At UHS, teachers who work most closely with Hmong students observed that in the last 10 years the age for marriage has increased among Hmong teens, and that fewer girls drop out of school to marry. Mrs. Quigley also noted that the number of Hmong girls becoming mothers during high school has also dropped in recent years.

As gender norms and roles have changed, so, too, have attitudes about ideal masculinity and femininity. Both the ideal Hmong boy and ideal Hmong girl of today embrace education as the road to economic security for the family. The new ideal boy/man respects his elders, speaks Hmong, and helps to care for his parents in their old age. Additionally, he is able to use his education and his knowledge of mainstream society to help his family negotiate life in the United States. Significantly, the younger generation of Hmong American leaders embody this new ideal masculinity. The ideal girl/woman, like the ideal boy/man, speaks Hmong, respects her elders, and understands the Hmong culture. The "good" Hmong girl also works hard in school and graduates from high school. Finally, the ideal Hmong girl/woman must remain sexually pure until she marries. It is important to note that American society is seen as being particularly threatening to female sexuality. Hmong parents fear that their daughters will adopt what they perceive to be the loose sexual mores of American society. Although the importance of sexual purity among girls is understood to be a traditional value, there is research that suggests premarital sex was not uncommon in Laos (Donnelly, 1994; Vang, 1982). If a girl got pregnant, it was understood that the boy was responsible for marrying her. Some researchers have asserted that the emphasis on the sexual purity of unmarried girls and women is the result of Christian influence (Barney, 1957).

The changing gender norms have led to some conflict between men and women and some conflict between generations. Some research, for example, suggests that Hmong men in the United States are struggling with a loss of status within Hmong families, a result of changing gender roles for women (Donnelly, 1994). Once the unquestioned authority in families, many Hmong men now find that they are dependent on their wives, their children, and the government (Donnelly, 1994). In her research on Hmong refugees in Seattle, Donnelly (1994) discovered that many Hmong men dreamed of returning to Laos, but Hmong women preferred life in the United States because they believed it offered greater gender equality for women. As noted earlier, Hmong parents are particularly concerned that their daughters will adapt American ideas regarding gender and sexuality. As Faderman and Xiong (1998) write, "Parents are horrified because they believe that one of their primary duties is to watch over a daughter carefully in order to protect her reputation, to make sure that she won't be considered sullied goods by potential in-laws" (p. 168).

At UHS, I found that young Hmong women regularly complained about gender inequality in their families and in Hmong culture. Jean's quote at the beginning of this chapter captures the feelings of many Hmong girls. By contrast, no young men reported being concerned about gender inequality. As Danny's quote at the beginning of the chapter suggests, many Hmong boys appear to view men's and women's work as separate but equal.

CONSTRUCTING HMONG FEMININITIES
IN THE UNITED STATES

All of the Hmong girls at UHS recognized that the dominant society views aspects of the Hmong culture as strange and problematic. Most of the young women were particularly sensitive to what mainstream Americans think about early marriage. Young women who were married hid their married status from UHS staff and their non-Hmong peers. Many of the young women would test my attitudes about early marriage by talking about girls they knew who were married or simply by asking me what I thought about high school–aged students getting married. I usually responded to the direct questions by saying something like, "I couldn't imagine being married in high school, but it really isn't my business. What do you think?" During lunch one day a Hmong student who was the mother of a 2-year-old complained that the doctors and nurses who delivered her baby treated her like "trash" because she was having a baby at the age of 14. As she told her story I noted that all of the young women at the table nodded in support of her outrage. Although they held varied opinions regarding when girls should marry and have children, most believed that early marriage was the business of the Hmong community and not the larger society.

While Hmong girls at UHS were sensitive to the ways the Hmong community is stereotyped by the dominant society, they all believed that mainstream American culture offered greater gender equality than Hmong culture. As I have already pointed out, the young women routinely complained about the gender inequality within Hmong families. The most common complaints were that as girls they had to stay home and do chores while their brothers were allowed to go out and didn't have any responsibilities. An examination of Hmong American Web sites and books written by the younger generation of Hmong American adults reveals that concerns regarding gender inequality in the Hmong culture are pervasive among girls and young women.

Traditional and Americanized females at UHS all assumed that American girls had more freedoms than they did. Their ideas regarding mainstream gender relations were gleaned from popular culture and from academic and social experiences at school. Scholars from various fields have observed the impact of popular culture on immigrant students' perceptions of gender relations in the United States (Olsen, 1997; Pyke, 2000). Popular images of the American family, in particular, are saturated with messages about gender and intergenerational relationships. In her study on the consumption of popular culture among Korean and Vietnamese immigrant youth, Pyke (2000) found that "public images of the Normal American Family constitute an ideological template that shapes respondents' familial perspectives and desires as new racial-ethnic Americans" (p. 240). Thus, popular images of the American family perpetuate the primacy of the White middle-class American family.

Young Hmong American women assumed that American (read: White) parents allowed their children to socialize freely with their friends and allowed them to go out on dates. Many Hmong females also believed that in American (read: White) families men and women shared household chores. Although Hmong girls usually used the term "American" to refer specifically to Whites, during these times African Americans were included as well. In general, Hmong girls assumed that most other ethnic groups experienced greater gender equality than they did. Both the young women described as traditional and those described as Americanized appeared to be largely unaware of the diversity among White families. Instead, they were confident that popular culture presented accurate representations of U.S. gender norms. Their unquestioning acceptance of the gender representations in popular culture suggests that schools need to engage students in critical media literacy.

Despite the fact that the Hmong girls at UHS shared a common concern about gender inequality in the Hmong culture and a common understanding that America offers greater gender equality, they expressed varied forms of femininity. They had different aspirations for their futures, different ideas regarding marriage, different relationships with their parents, and different styles of dress and self-presentation. The various expressions of femininity intersect in complicated ways with the traditional and Americanized categories of Hmong students.

Traditional Young Women

Young women who described themselves and were described by others as traditional were the ones most likely to be viewed as being "good" by the Hmong American community. ESL teachers and others who worked closely with these students identified them as the "un-Americanized" girls who needed support and guidance in negotiating U.S. gender norms. Traditional young women follow school rules and embrace education as the route to economic security. In fact, traditional girls were among the most successful Hmong students at UHS. They were more likely to make the honor roll, to participate in compensatory educational programs aimed at college-bound students, and to have close relationships with their teachers than traditional boys, Americanized boys, or Americanized girls. During my research at UHS I only knew of one Hmong student who went on to attend a highly selective university, and this student was a traditional young woman.

While traditional girls outperformed all Hmong boys at UHS, it is important to point out that data from the 2000 census shows that Hmong women continue to lag behind Hmong men in educational attainment (Vang, 2004; Yang & Pfeifer, 2004). Interestingly, the Hmong community perceives Hmong women as becoming more successful in higher education than Hmong men (Vang, 2004). Although the census data and the perceptions of the Hmong community may appear to be at odds, I would suggest otherwise. The census data reflects the fact that Hmong men are more likely to persist in school. This makes sense since some Hmong girls continue to leave school in order to marry and have children. Although attitudes regarding early marriage vary within the Hmong community, there is still more pressure on girls than on boys to marry at relatively young ages. Educational persistence, however, is not the same thing as high achievement, and it is possible that the Hmong community has observed women to be the highest achievers. In short, the Hmong community may be observing the same trend of high achievement among girls and women that I observed at UHS.

In my previous work on Hmong American women who pursued undergraduate and graduate degrees, I discovered that high achievement among Hmong women was in part a response to cultural norms regarding gender. Hmong American women explained that Hmong men could get respect with or without an education, but education was one of the only ways for women to gain freedom (Lee, 1997). Similarly, the high-achieving Hmong American young women at UHS explain that education is a way to gain personal independence and to escape lives like the ones led by their mothers.

The academic success of traditional Hmong American young women may, at first glance, appear to be somewhat surprising, since Hmong culture has been described as highly patriarchal. Here, the concept of a positive dual frame of reference is helpful. According to Ogbu (1987), immigrants possess a positive dual frame of reference whereby they compare their opportunities and situations in the United States with those in their native countries and conclude that life is better in the United States. As I stated previously, Hmong girls uniformly believed that there are greater opportunities for women in the United States than in Laos. Traditional young women, in particular, were grateful for the perceived opportunities in the United States, especially the existence of free public education. Most traditional girls were still in ESL classes, where they received the support of White female educators who were committed to assisting them to attain greater gender equality through education. Traditional girls also viewed Mrs. Her as a role model. These young women interpreted the fact that Mrs. Her was pursuing an undergraduate degree as evidence that they, too, could pursue higher education.

Although traditional young women talked about a desire for increased gender equality within their families, they tended to accept their parents' authority. They seemed to believe that the images of relative gender equality reflected in popular cultural representations of the American family were out of reach for them. Thus, they performed household chores with little resistance and followed their parents' wishes regarding marriage. During my fieldwork at UHS, the two cases of arranged marriage that I heard about involved young women who described themselves as being traditional. One young woman told me that she cried for days and days when her parents told her that they had arranged her marriage. She said that she begged them not to force her to marry until she was finished with school. This student was well aware that in the United States her parents could not legally force her to marry. She knew that if social welfare workers learned of her situation, her parents could get into trouble and she could be removed from their care. Ultimately this young woman decided that her parents loved her and had her best interests in mind, and so she agreed to the marriage. Thus, traditional girls may assent to arranged marriage out of respect and obligation to parents. By assenting to an arranged marriage, the aforementioned young woman ensured that her family and culture were protected from the interference of outsiders.

May, whom I introduced in chapter 3, is an example of a self-defined traditional young woman. When I first arrived at UHS, May was identified by two teachers and one vice principal as an excellent example of a hard-working, smart, and serious Hmong student. The very first time I met May she proudly asserted that her dream was to go on to college when she graduated from UHS. May routinely made the honor roll, was a member of the junior varsity math team, and participated in a compensatory education program for low-income students. She was in the ESL program during her ninth-grade year and was transitioning into mainstream classes during her 10th-grade year. According to May, her parents have always encouraged her to do well in school, and they support her educational aspirations. Like other traditional young women, May wears her hair long and straight and dresses in conservative clothing. She is fluent in Hmong and performs Hmong dances at Hmong community events. Most importantly, May's willingness to obey her parents' rules, perform household chores, and take care of her younger siblings makes her a "good" daughter and a "good Hmong girl." She explained that good daughters also stay away from boys and remain "pure." She also stated that she was more than happy to comply with her parents' rules because she was focusing on her studies. Although May gets along well with her parents, she reported that she often fights with her younger, "more Americanized sister," who makes fun of her for being "too traditional."

While it may appear that the traditional young women really are simply traditional, it is more accurate to say that they are following their parents' lead in selectively acculturating to U.S. cultural norms that they perceive to be necessary for mainstream success (Gibson, 1988; Portes & Rumbaut, 2001). The education of girls and women, for example, does not reflect a traditional Hmong value, but the Hmong community has embraced education for girls and women and has reframed education through high school as being consistent with traditional Hmong ideas. Traditional young women remarked that education is, in fact, a way to gain greater gender equality because it will bring them economic independence. Furthermore, while traditional young women may follow their parents' ways out of respect, many assert that they will raise their own children in "Hmong and American ways." For example, they frequently asserted that they would teach their children to value gender equality. Finally, they routinely stated that they would encourage their daughters to postpone marriage until they were finished with their educations.

Americanized Young Women

Scholarship on youth has pointed to the symbolic use of clothing and music to define group membership (Eckert, 1989). During my early fieldwork I assumed that the Americanized young women represented a relatively monolithic group because they share a common style. As noted in the previous chapter, Americanized girls purchased and wore clothes that teachers and non-Hmong students associated with Black urban youth. Unlike traditional girls, who did not wear makeup, Americanized girls often applied lipstick, eye makeup, and foundation. Some of them lightened their hair and wore blue and green contact lenses in what appeared to be efforts to whiten their appearance. In fact, hair bleaching and the wearing of colored contact lenses appear to be common among Asian American girls and women from various ethnic backgrounds (Lee & Vaught, 2003; Moua, 2002). Americanized girls also shared a common belief that the decisions regarding marriage should be left to the individual girl, and they rejected any suggestion that the dominant society should have any say about marriage in the Hmong community.

Despite these similarities, however, I discovered that distinctions within the Americanized girls did exist. Those who described themselves as Americanized represented a diverse group in terms of their attitudes toward marriage, relationships with parents, and attitudes toward the role of education in their lives. They can be divided into two groups. The first group of Americanized girls are viewed by fellow Hmong students and Hmong adults as "good girls." These girls are seen as having maintained aspects of the Hmong culture. The second group of Americanized girls are characterized by their peers and Hmong adults as being "bad girls" or over-Americanized. Differences within these two groups also exist, but I found that within each group the young women share certain characteristics.

Aside from differences in clothing styles and makeup, the first group of Americanized girls were very similar to the traditional girls in that they conformed to school rules by regularly attending their classes, doing their homework, and staying out of trouble. Although some of these young women might occasionally challenge or question Hmong cultural norms, they generally obey their parents, perform household chores, and take care of their younger siblings. These young women also obey their parents' rules regarding contact with boys. In short, they are "good" daughters and "good Hmong girls."

Blia, a senior in the class of 1999, is an example of this first type of Americanized girl. With her long black hair, dramatic black eyeliner, dark lipstick, and tight jeans, Blia is a striking figure. Blia proudly reported that she had been a contestant in the Miss Hmong Wisconsin pageant. According to Blia, contestants in the Miss Hmong pageant should be beautiful and must be able to demonstrate knowledge of Hmong and American cultures. Like many Hmong American girls, Blia was interested in my marital status. She was particularly interested in my Chinese background and my knowledge and connection to Chinese culture. She nodded in appreciation when I told her that my mother had been strict when I was a teenager, and appeared visibly shocked when she learned that many of my cousins remained unmarried into their thirties. We often spoke about gender relations in my family, and she was impressed to learn that my mother always worked outside the home.

A hard-working student, Blia planned to pursue her associate's degree upon graduating from high school. As a "good Hmong girl," Blia followed her mother's rules regarding dating. Her boyfriend visited her at her house, and her mother or sister accompanied them on their dates. Blia explained that although she wanted to spend time alone with her boyfriend, she would not consider breaking the rules because it would threaten her own and her family's reputation. She explained that her ability to marry well was connected to her behavior as a "good Hmong girl."

Blia's beliefs regarding marriage reflected her efforts to find a balance between the aspects of American culture she enjoyed and the aspects of Hmong culture she hoped to preserve. Blia reported that she didn't want to marry too young, but she also feared waiting until she was too old, which she defined as being over 20. Interestingly, Blia's concerns regarding the fear of "being too old" appear to come from the Hmong peer culture and not the parent generation. Mrs. Her observed:

> I guess there is some kind of pressure [to get married]. Maybe not at home, but the girl just feel she needs to get married. I think I'm seeing now, in the case of girls who are in the mainstream [i.e., not in ESL classes], they feel that they are, they need to get married because they're getting old and whatever.

Mrs. Her notes that the young women get many of their ideas regarding the appropriate age for marriage by watching the experiences of older female siblings and cousins. Referring to her own experiences, she says:

For example, in my generation, even the men who are, who finish college, who has a master's degree, I mean, they will come back and marry girls who's, oh geez, I cannot, um, teenager girls, instead of choosing a girl who's finished college, I mean who has a good education, a job.

Mrs. Her's comments point to the role that peer culture has on the formation of gender identity (Holland & Eisenhart, 1991; Thorne, 1993).

Blia is interested in marrying a man who reflects both Hmong cultural norms and some mainstream American cultural norms. The following conversation captures Blia's ideas regarding the ideal husband:

> SL: What are you looking for in a husband?
> Blia: Well, I'm looking for nothing too, nothing like . . . I want him to be kind of traditional, but then modern.
> SL: Can you say more about that?
> Blia: Like, he has, like he knows Hmong, Hmong ways, but still have (sic) an open mind to think modern.
> SL: What kinds of things are important for him to be open-minded about, do you think?
> Blia: Um, like Hmong traditions. He should, like we should like have an agreement on which ones are to follow and which ones aren't. And like modern, like he's still like he has an open mind on like women's, what women can do.

Blia went on to explain that she would respect her future husband's authority as the man of the house, but she also wants him to respect and listen to her opinions.

Blia plans to teach both her sons and daughters to help around the house. She explained that as the oldest daughter she has had to take care of her younger siblings, cook the meals, and help her mother in the family garden. With a slight note of irritation in her voice, she noted that her brothers don't do anything around the house. Ultimately, however, Blia doesn't blame her brothers because she sees their behavior as being tied to a traditional male upbringing. She is confident that she will be able to achieve gender equality among her future children by following the lessons about gender roles that she has learned from TV.

> Blia: I would have, like I would have set chores for my kids.
> SL: For boys and girls?
> Blia: Yeah, like I would like make a chart and have them like do their thing, and when they're done, you can like check it off or whatever.

SL: Where did you get that idea?

Blia: I've seen it in the movies. And like some families, Hmong
families do that now, and it works well.

Six months after she graduated from high school, I ran into Blia at the
Hmong New Year's celebration, and she gave me a big hug and reported
that she had gotten married to her longtime boyfriend. She described it as
a "love" marriage that was approved by both families. Blia stated that she
still planned to continue her education and that her husband supports her
desire to go to school.

Moua Y. (discussed in chapter 3) is another example of an Americanized girl who has managed to stay within the boundaries of being a "good"
daughter and a "good Hmong girl." Moua has also been influenced by
popular cultural images of gender relations in American families. Here she
reflects on her image of the mainstream family:

> And the kids are doing house chores and everything, they like have
> good grades and even when the girl grows up, the woman, the
> mom has a good job like a doctor of something. And the father
> supports the girls, she may go to college to be a doctor or major in
> business or something and the dad totally support it.

As her quote suggests, Moua's believes that gender equality is common to
the American family. Particularly salient is her belief that American fathers support their daughters in their pursuit of education and professional
occupations. Moua Y. wishes that her parents were more like the families
that she sees on TV, and she explains that she often argues with her mother
about the gender inequality between the girls and the boys in her family.

> I really hate it because I guess they [parents] are kind of stuck in
> their own . . . they are kind of stuck in how things used to be, you
> know? The guys do the work—go to work, and the girls do the
> house chores and stuff. So um . . . my mom still does house chore
> stuff, me and my sister still does that, and my dad, he doesn't do
> that cause he has like two jobs, you know. He's always tired. But
> then my brothers, they don't do anything, which gets me really
> upset. Every time, every time my mom tells us to like do the
> laundry I am always fighting. "No—I am not doing their laundry,
> they are old enough to do their laundry."

Although she occasionally voices her discontent regarding gender norms
in her family, Moua Y. explains that she does the chores, including her

brothers' laundry, because she is expected to do so. She notes that she would feel guilty if she didn't obey her parents' rules. Like the traditional students, Moua feels obligated to her parents for the sacrifices they have made for their children. She is acutely aware of her mother's hard work on behalf of the family and therefore performs the household chores in order to help relieve her mother's burdens.

With respect to the issue of marriage, Moua Y. is adamant that she will not marry until she finishes college and gets a job. She believes that "high school is too young to get married." Moua explained that her parents "aren't too strict or too traditional" compared to other Hmong parents because they do not encourage early marriage and they support education for girls. Her parents have emphasized that early marriage does not make good economic sense in the United States. Moua's older sister and role model is unmarried and attending college in California, and her parents have told her that she can pursue a college education as long as she "stays away from boys."

Although Blia and Moua Y. have different ideas regarding the appropriate age for marriage, they are both staying within the shifting boundaries of Hmong cultural norms regarding gender. Their ideas regarding gender relations are influenced by popular culture, but neither young woman disregards parental authority in efforts to achieve the idealized gender norms represented in popular culture. Both girls are motivated by a sense of obligation to their parents (Suarez-Orozco, 1989). Most significantly, both girls have maintained their identities as "good girls" by following their parents' standards concerning sexuality. Like the girls described as traditional, those described as being "Americanized in a good way" are practicing a selective acculturation that is approved by the adults in the Hmong American community (Gibson, 1988; Portes & Rumbaut, 2001). While the Hmong American community appears to value both Moua Y.'s and Blia's expressions of femininity, Moua's interest in postponing marriage until after college fits more closely with UHS's notion of "normal" femininity (i.e., White and middle class).

While some Americanized girls' expressions of femininity were consistent with the gender ideals of the larger Hmong American community, a growing number of Hmong American girls at UHS were expressing forms of femininity that Hmong adults view as problematic. These young women were seen as "Americanizing in a bad way" and turning into "bad girls." This second group of Americanized girls often resisted their parents' authority and resisted what they perceived to be the restrictive gender norms in their families. They longed for the freedom that their brothers enjoyed and coveted the freedom that they assumed non-Hmong girls enjoyed. Some of these girls refused to perform household chores, leaving their mothers or "good girl" sisters to do all the cooking and cleaning. Girls in this group were also the most likely to resist the authority of the school and cut classes. Teachers and other school authorities referred to these girls as "Americanizing in bad ways" (read: non-White ways). Like other young women of color, these Americanized Hmong girls were seen as being at risk. The problems that these young women had in school also contributed to the intergenerational conflict in their families.

The biggest source of conflict between these girls and their parents, however, involved the issue of dating and sexuality. While parents insist that "good girls" either stay away from boys or date under the watchful eyes of the family, this group of Americanized girls was interested in exploring what they referred to as "less traditional," "more modern," and "more Americanized" relationships with boys. Their adoption of mainstream ideas about dating leads to their characterization as "bad girls." According to the Hmong community, "bad girls" risk their chances for a "good marriage" and ruin the reputations of their families (Ngo, 2002). In desperate attempts to preserve their daughters' reputations, some families send their "bad daughters" to live with relatives in order to remove them from bad influences (Ngo, 2002). At UHS I knew of one Americanized girl who was living with her aunt's family because her parents had sent her away. In conversations with Americanized youth I learned that this was an increasingly common practice within the Hmong community.

The connection between family reputation and a daughter's sexual purity is common to other Asian immigrant groups (Gibson, 1988; Smith-Hefner, 1999). Some research suggests that the obsession with daughters' sexual purity becomes exaggerated in the United States because immigrants fear the loss of control over their lives. From this perspective, the protection of female honor is not simply an expression of tradition, but a response to perceptions of threats of the host society. As noted earlier, for example, premarital sex was not entirely taboo in Laos (Vang, 1982).

When this second group of Americanized girls talks about relationships with boys, they focus on the importance of romantic love and individual choice. Specifically, they dream of meeting the right man, dating free of parental interference, and falling in love. Their ideas about dating and love are informed by romance fiction, soap operas, and movies. Young women who rarely read school assignments would often carry around romance fiction to read during lunch or study hall. In her research on immigrant high school students, Olsen (1997) also discovered that first- and second-generation immigrant girls learned from popular culture the mainstream expectations for gender and femininity that emphasized dating and romance. In addition to shaping ideas about romance, popular culture appeared to shape the girls' ideas about the ideal man. This group of Americanized girls, for example, often complained within earshot of their male peers that "Hmong guys are short." They all remarked that "taller Hmong guys are cuter" than short ones. These young Hmong women and the young Hmong men who are the victims of these messages have internalized the idea that being short is seen as a feminine characteristic by the dominant American society (Lei, 2003).

Several of these Americanized girls spoke about meeting boyfriends over the Internet in various Hmong chat rooms. They noted that the Internet allows them to become acquainted with their boyfriends without their parents' knowledge. Once they established a relationship over the Internet, these young women would go to considerable effort to arrange clandestine face-to-face meetings. Sneaking around behind their parents' backs, however, is not without risks. For a girl who has been sexually active, marriage is often seen as the only viable option, and the threat of marriage is used as a form of control. During a lunchroom conversation with Hmong youth, several students joked that "If you don't want to get married, don't fool around." The bilingual resource specialist, Mrs. Her, explained the parents' perspective in the following way:

> In Hmong culture . . . the girls are not supposed to go out with boys. And if you're going, if you go out with a boy more than a couple of hours, then usually the parents don't want you back. Even if it's during the daytime and it's worse during the nighttime.

As Mrs. Her's comments suggest, girls are more vulnerable to the pressures of forced marriage than boys. Hope, who fits into this second group of Americanized young women, elaborated:

> Forced marriage? I don't like. Forced marriage is really easy to get. If you, if your parents at home and you have a, let's say—Okay, I'm going out with somebody and his parents ain't home. And I just stayed up in his—we're up in his room, just talking, whatever. You could get forced marriage by that.

As Hope's and Mrs. Her's comments suggest, the power of gossip can determine a girl's future. Those who are accused of engaging in sexual relations are often simply assumed to be guilty, and forced marriage may be the consequence. As is common among groups that place a great deal of emphasis on female sexual purity, Hmong parents also use forced marriage to deter the possibility of bad behavior on the part of daughters who are identified as being at risk for inappropriate behavior (Gibson, 1988; Smith-Hefner, 1999).

Interestingly, I found that some of the Americanized girls in this second group chose marriage even when their parents tried to dissuade them. Those who experience high levels of intergenerational conflict with their parents use marriage as a culturally sanctioned form of resistance to parental control and authority. In her research on Hmong American college students, Ngo (2002) observed a similar trend whereby women engaged in early marriage as a way to defy parental control. At UHS, young women who were married were careful to hide their married status from school officials for fear of moral and sometimes legal judgment. In this case, silence should be read as a form of resistance to school and other dominant authorities. Americanized girls who are alienated from school also view early marriage as an excuse to drop out of school and resist the controlling authority of school. Although these young women assume that marriage will grant them greater freedom, Mrs. Her points out that most young married Hmong couples live with the husband's family, leaving the daughter-in-law under her in-laws' control.

Mai is an example of a girl who fits into this second category of Americanized girls. Mai typically dressed in tight-fitting bell-bottom jeans, cropped T-shirts or sweaters, and chunky platform shoes. She was one of the only Hmong girls to wear her hair shorter than shoulder-length. As noted earlier, hair is political, and Mai was purposely wearing her hair in a style that she described as "more Americanized." Loquacious and energetic, Mai often flirted with Hmong and non-Hmong boys. Her behavior and dress reflect her desire to emulate the behavior of the "typical" teen she has seen represented in popular culture. Dating and having fun were central to her understanding of typical teen activities. During a lunchtime conversation Mai proclaimed that girls officially become teens and begin to explore intimate relationships with boys when they turn 13. As Mai related her opinions on adolescence, her Americanized girlfriends nodded and laughed in agreement. Mai (14 at the time) remembered that at 13 she had her first boyfriend and her first kiss. She added quickly, however, that her parents still do not know that she has had boyfriends and would be furious if they ever found out. An avid reader of romance fiction, Mai relies on the naturalized images of adolescence gleaned from popular culture in order to justify the fact that she sneaks around her parents' backs.

Like others who were in this group of Americanized students, Mai met her boyfriends over the Internet. Although meeting boys over the Internet may sound very Americanized and therefore not culturally Hmong, it is important to point out that the Americanized youth called upon their Hmong cultural norms in their Internet encounters. "What is your last name?" is among the first things that Mai and other Hmong students ask people they meet in Hmong chat rooms. One informant explained simply that it is important to know whether the person in the chat room is a cousin. If they share a last name they are understood to be cousins and therefore inappropriate for dating. Internet users also inquire about the religious background of the other party. Hmong who are Christian prefer other Christian Hmong, and those who practice traditional Hmong religious beliefs prefer traditional Hmong. Technology even allows students to "check each other out" and see whether there is mutual attraction. Thus, the Internet provides students with a way to engage in virtual dating under their parents' eyes.

Sia is another example of a girl who is Americanized in ways that the Hmong community and the UHS staff view as problematic. When I first met her she defiantly announced that she lived with her Hmong boyfriend. Months later Sia's friends revealed that she had been married "in the Hmong tradition" for the last couple of years. The girls' reference to marriage "in the Hmong tradition" meant that Sia and her husband had participated in the Hmong marriage ceremony, but had not yet become legally married. I was surprised to learn this because I had spent a great deal of time with Sia, and I had assumed that we had a fairly good relationship. When I asked her about being married she emphasized that she was not legally married, but "only married in the Hmong tradition." The fact that she hid her marital status from me was yet another piece of evidence regarding the political nature of marriage. I would argue that Sia hid her marital status because she wanted to present herself in a way that was more consistent with her perceptions of American societal norms. While many non-Hmong teens have boyfriends, few have husbands, and Sia appeared to recognize this. Like other married Hmong girls, Sia was engaging in impression management (Kolytk, 1998).

As I spoke more to Sia it became clear that she had chosen to marry her husband as a way to resist her parents' authority and the authority of the school. Sia was estranged from her parents, who she explained did not really know her, and alienated from school authorities, whom she perceived to be uncaring. The tension between Sia and her parents was exacerbated by her unquestioning acceptance of the White family ideal represented in popular culture (Pyke, 2000). As Sia said,

> Well I guess they always have those TV shows with the perfect family, and. . . . And you know, you do kind of envy that. I mean, you don't have it . . . I don't know, but like, I like wish I had a good family. For me, I think that's why a lot of white people are successful, you know?

Sia dreams of starting a family with her husband that will mirror the families she watches on TV.

Zer is a third example who fits into this second group of American-ized young women. While Zer typically dressed in hip-hop–style clothes, she also aspired to and had internalized a standard of extreme thinness associated with the White middle-class gender aesthetic. Prior to hearing Zer talk about dieting, I had mistakenly assumed that young Hmong women at UHS were largely unconcerned with their weight. In my early observations, it appeared that most of the Hmong American girls at UHS were fairly comfortable with their bodies regardless of their size. Until Zer's comments I had never heard any of the young women discuss the calo-ries, fat content, or carbohydrates in their food. I had assumed that the girls' relatively healthy body images were linked to beauty standards in Laos, where full-figured women were prized in the Hmong community because their size was equated with fecundity (Lynch, 1999). When I asked Zer and her friends about their desire to lose weight, they reported that they wanted to look more like the actresses they saw on TV. They explained that many Hmong young women were beginning to worry about weight because boys "don't like fat girls." Most surprising was Zer's assertion that many Hmong parents value thinness in women because they recognize that thin women are valued in the dominant U.S. culture. After this con-versation with Zer, I asked some of the other Americanized girls, includ-ing those who were identified as "good," and I found that an alarming number of young women were expressing concern about their weight.

Like Sia, Zer has also internalized beliefs about the supposed superi-ority of White families. While Sia continues to find Hmong men attrac-tive, Zer asserted, "I want to want to marry an American [White]. I'd kill myself if I had to marry a Hmong guy." In fact, Zer explained that the only reason she wasn't more worried about her weight was because she was uninterested in the boys at UHS. Zer was among those most likely to hurl demeaning comments at Hmong boys, who she described as "wimpy and short." Espiritu (2000) argues that the gendered and sexualized stereo-types of Asian Americans have had a profoundly negative impact on rela-tionships between Asian American men and women. She states, "Due to the persistent de-sexualization of the Asian male, many Asian females do not perceive their ethnic counterparts as desirable marriage partners" (p. 97). One day during lunch Zer asked me whether I had any family members who were married to White people. When I told her that my mother's brother is married to a White woman, she asked, "Are your cousins cute? Mixed people are always cute." As Zer waxed on about the supposed superiority of White physical features, I was reminded of simi-lar comments made by my relatives. The assumptions regarding the physi-cal attractiveness of mixed-raced Asians (read: White and Asian) reflect one of the hidden injuries of racism (Osajima, 1991).

CONSTRUCTING HMONG MASCULINITIES
IN THE UNITED STATES

Hmong American boys at UHS recognize that White boys/men hold the racialized and gendered power at the school and in the larger society. Furthermore, they realize that as Hmong American boys they lack the qualities associated with hegemonic masculinity. While Hmong American girls believe that there are greater opportunities for them as girls/women in the United States than there would be in Laos, Hmong American males' status as boys/men is challenged by dominant definitions of masculinity. Hmong boys must contend with the fact that some Americanized Hmong girls are not attracted to Hmong boys, who are described as being "too short." In addition to negotiating dominant messages about masculinity, Hmong American boys must also negotiate the Hmong American community's messages about masculinity. "Good Hmong sons" must do well in school, help their parents, and understand Hmong cultural norms. The Hmong American boys at UHS express a variety of masculinities in response to the messages about gender that they gather at home and at school.

Traditional Young Men

Most of the young men who are described as being traditional are relative newcomers to the United States and are still uncertain about some mainstream cultural practices, and this keeps them from engaging in school activities. Their understandings of masculinity are drawn from what they have learned from their fathers, grandfathers, and other elders. These boys wear relatively nondescript clothes that are chosen for practicality rather than fashion. In contrast to White boys at UHS who express hegemonic masculinity, the traditional young men take up little actual or figurative space in the school. They occupy the sidelines in the cafeteria, the halls, and the classrooms. In many respects, these young men are the quintessential examples of the quiet (i.e., harmless) Hmong boys described by some teachers. Americanized girls, in particular, mocked these boys for being "nerds."

As a self-described "traditional Hmong," Cha believes that it is important to respect his elders and carry on other Hmong cultural practices. Cha explained that "traditional Hmong sons" help to care for their parents in their old age, and he intends to live up to this responsibility. Cha lives with his mother in a low-income housing development in Lakeview. Cha explained that his father had several wives and decided to stay in Laos with one of his wives and their children. Because his father is still in Laos, Cha is already responsible for helping to support his mother. Cha works nearly

40 hours a week at a grocery store after school and on weekends in order to help pay the family bills. Because of his work schedule, Cha gets home late on most school nights and is often too tired to do his homework. Between a work schedule that prevents him from studying long hours and his difficulties with English, Cha struggles in a few of his classes. Although Cha has taken on the family responsibilities associated with being a "traditional Hmong son," these very responsibilities interfere with his schoolwork. Despite his language difficulties, however, Cha receives at least passing grades because of his effort and attitude. Although he would like to pursue a 2-year vocational education degree upon graduating from high school, he is afraid that his financial responsibilities for his mother will make it impossible for him to pay for school.

Sometime in the next few years Cha wants to marry a Hmong woman who shares his cultural values. While his father has several wives, he asserted that he only wants one wife. He is interested in marrying his current girlfriend, but he is not sure that she will want to marry him since she plans to go to college after she graduates from high school. In contrast to other self-described "traditional Hmong men" who do not want to marry educated women, Cha is supportive of his girlfriend's interest in pursuing postsecondary education. Cha is also afraid that his girlfriend's family does not like him because he is not from a well-respected and prominent family. Because his father is still in Laos, his family is left outside the circle of power in the Hmong American community.

Although most traditional young men work hard and believe in the achievement ideology, their limited English-language skills will most likely restrict their mainstream success. The Hmong American community looks toward the next generation of Hmong Americans to serve as cultural bridges between the Hmong American community and the larger American society, and those who can successfully negotiate both Hmong culture and mainstream American culture will likely be the future leaders of the Hmong American community. Due to limited English language skills, it is unlikely that Cha will become a leader in the Hmong American community.

"Good Americanization": A New Ideal Masculinity for the Hmong Americans

Some members of the younger generation of Hmong men are attempting to construct a masculinity that reflects, combines, and reinterprets aspects of the hegemonic masculinity valued by the dominant society with aspects of the masculinity valued by Hmong culture. As noted above, these men can negotiate both mainstream American society and the Hmong American community. Many of the younger Hmong leaders embody this expression of masculinity, suggesting that this represents the new ideal Hmong American masculinity that parents encourage in their sons. Hmong boys and men who reflect this type of masculinity speak Hmong, demonstrate respect for elders, and understand other Hmong cultural norms, but they are also comfortable negotiating mainstream society and have achieved a certain level of educational success. Although this new ideal Hmong American masculinity shares things in common with the hegemonic masculinity of the dominant society, it should not be confused with the hegemonic masculinity of the school or of the larger society because it is also in conversation with the values and beliefs of the Hmong community.

Kao is one example of a Hmong American young man who expresses the "good" Americanization associated with the new ideal masculinity in the Hmong American community. Kao is also one of a few Hmong boys who managed to establish comfortable and friendly relationships with both male and female members of the UHS staff. He appeared to be completely comfortable with the authority of female teachers and administrators. Kao was even on a first-name basis with Mrs. Schultz, the school's head principal. Unlike most of his Hmong male peers, Kao embodies some of the qualities associated with the hegemonic masculinity of the school. One member of the guidance office described Kao as a "good kid" and a "successful student." Kao is the president of the Asian Club and a member of the student senate, and is on the track and gymnastics teams. In addition to participating in several extracurricular activities, Kao maintains a B average in school. In contrast to most of the Americanized boys at UHS, who wore hip-hop–style clothes, Kao emulated the fashion of the more conservative White middle-class youth at the school. Aware that his clothes made a social statement, Kao described his style as "preppy."

Perhaps most significantly, Kao's decisions regarding how and with whom to spend his time set him apart from most of the Hmong American boys at the school. While most Hmong boys only socialized with Hmong or other Southeast Asian youth, Kao associates primarily with White students he knows through participating in school-sponsored sports or other extracurricular activities. In addition to his White friends, Kao is friendly with a number of Asian American (non-Hmong) students he knows through the Asian Club and with a few African American students he knows from his work on multicultural events at the school. Kao explained that he made a conscious decision to separate himself from other Hmong American youth.

> When I was younger, I used to hang out with a lot of Hmong people. And I didn't get much done. I just usually do what they did and just played around a lot. And I guess, now, I just want to better

myself, so I try, try not to hang out with the Hmong people a lot. Just because, somehow, I see them as not trying hard enough, so I try not to hang out with them.

Thus, Kao's decision to distance himself from other Hmong youth was based on his desire to learn about the dominant American culture and to improve his future life chances. He views the adoption of certain aspects of White masculinity as being imperative for mainstream success. Kao asserted that his decision to socialize with White students has allowed him to learn about the larger society, but he also recognized that his choice was not without cost. As a Hmong American student in a largely White social clique, Kao said he is "more accepted than most Hmong people," but he also knows that his race and ethnicity mark him as being different from the rest of the group. There have been occasions, for example, when he has witnessed the way non-Asian students stereotype Asian students. Although his friends try to reassure him by telling him that he is "different from most other Asian kids," this leaves Kao feeling "good and bad." He realizes that his acceptance by the dominant group is contingent upon his willingness to play by their rules, specifically the rules of White hegemonic masculinity. Significantly, because Kao is not White he can never actually achieve the hegemonic masculinity of the school.

Although Kao distances himself from most other Hmong boys at the school, he does not distance himself from Hmong adults or the Hmong culture. In fact, he maintains a strong Hmong identity. Kao criticizes the Hmong American boys at UHS for being "very nontraditional" in their attitudes toward the Hmong elders in the community. He argues that while most Hmong students isolate themselves socially, they also "try and draw away from Hmong culture." He suggested that most of his Hmong American peers had "Americanized in bad ways." Interestingly, Kao reported that his parents warned him to keep his distance from "Hmong kids who were Americanized in bad ways."

Kao asserted that he was proud to be Hmong and that he tried to make his parents proud by being a "good Hmong son." Kao explained that "good Hmong sons" dress conservatively and specifically not "like a gangster." He went on to explain that Hmong adults assumed that when Hmong kids wore baggy clothes it meant they were involved with gangs. Thus, Kao's relatively conservative clothing style reflects his desire to please his parents and to fit in with the dominant culture. He also explained that "good Hmong sons" are expected to "be respectful of others, elders, get a good education, etc." Interestingly, "good sons" are those who reflect a combination of traditional characteristics (e.g., respectful of elders) with acculturated characteristics (e.g., formally educated). Regarding the importance of education for social mobility, Kao explained that his parents want their children "to be in a better position than they are now—financial-wise." Kao noted that while his parents encouraged his sisters to do well in school, they have paid particular attention to his and his brother's education because the sons are expected to remain close to the parents and help them in their old age. Thus, Kao's family, like other Hmong families, views the education of sons as an investment for the family.

Like his older brother, Kao plans to attend a 2-year technical college and then transfer to a 4-year university. Upon earning his 4-year degree, Kao dreams of marrying a Hmong American woman, buying a house, and starting a family. In short, Kao's plans bear a resemblance to the "American dream." He believes that associating with White Americans will help him gain access to information and resources necessary for economic and social advancement. Although he seeks individual achievement, he plans to use his achievements to help his parents. In other words, individual achievement in school is understood to be in the service of the extended family. As a "good Hmong son," he believes that it is essential for him to support his parents in their old age. He dreams of raising his children, who will be third-generation Hmong Americans, with a sense of their Hmong heritage and a connection to their paternal grandparents. In short, by being a "good son" Kao is achieving the new ideal masculinity of the Hmong American community.

Michael is another example of a Hmong American who fit the mold of a "good Americanized" young man. During my first weeks at UHS, several members of the staff suggested that I speak with Michael. He was consistently described as a "good kid" who was "on track academically" and "involved in the school." Michael explained that he got along with most of his teachers and found them to be helpful and supportive about his educational aspirations. Like other Hmong American students, he liked educators who demonstrated that they cared about him as a person. He described Mr. Buckner, one of his favorite adults at UHS, like this: " I mean he's cool, he'd just talk to you, ordinary. Like, as if you were a good friend and not like a teacher, make you feel comfortable."

Michael was a member of the school's gymnastics team, cross-country team, and track team. He joined the gymnastics team at Kao's encouragement. During his senior year Michael was a member of the school's multicultural theater group. He explained that he joined the theater group because his former ESL counselor suggested that it would be a good experience for him. At the end of his senior year the director of the multicultural theater group asked Michael to recruit a Hmong American student to be in the group the following year, but he was unable to find anyone who was interested. According to Michael, most Hmong students simply do not feel comfortable performing in front of "Americans." Although Michael knew students from different ethnic and racial backgrounds through his involvement in extracurricular activities, he could usually be found socializing with other Americanized Hmong students. He explained that he was simply "more comfortable with Hmong."

Michael earned B's and C's at UHS, but was quick to point out that he got better grades in middle school before the academic work got more difficult. He plans to go to technical college for 2 years and then transfer to a university to earn a B.A. In discussing his parents' dreams for him, Michael stated, "They want me to be a doctor. You know how parents are—doctor, lawyer, and stuff like that." When I asked him why his parents want him to be a doctor, Michael elaborated, "Well, it's better, you get respect. Higher respect, higher pay. You're rich. And stuff like that." Michael assumes that he will marry a Hmong woman after he graduates from college. His dream is to have a good job, a house in the country, and a family of his own. As a son, he knows that it will also be his responsibility to help take care of his parents and he plans to do just that.

It is important to note that Kao and Michael embody the type of masculinity expressed by the new generation of Hmong American leaders. Like many of the new generation of Hmong American leaders in communities throughout the United States, Kao and Michael view education as the route to social mobility. While this new generation of Hmong leaders has internalized the dominant achievement ideology, they are also committed to maintaining a distinct Hmong identity. In short, these young men have adopted the strategy of accommodation without assimilation whereby they adopt aspects of the dominant culture without losing their ethnic identities and cultures (Gibson, 1988). Many of the new Hmong American leaders use their educational backgrounds to work on behalf of Hmong American communities.

"Bad Americanization" and Counterhegemonic Masculinity

In contrast to young men like Kao and Michael are those who express a counterhegemonic masculinity that resists the hegemonic masculinity advanced by the school and the dominant society, and the new ideal masculinity of the Hmong American community (Lynch, 1999). These boys reject the authority of the school, question the role of education in social mobility, and question their parents' authority. They were the group of Hmong American students least likely to approach UHS staff, particularly female members of the staff, for assistance. These young men are the ones most likely to dress and talk in hip-hop styles as a way to resist racial inequality and to resist the image that Asian men lack masculinity. They adopt the "cool pose"—swagger, posture—associated with African American men (Dance, 2002; Kelley, 1997). Many of these Americanized boys practiced break dancing in the halls, thereby claiming space in the schools (Kelley, 1997). Assumed to be gang members, these young men are blackened in the dominant discourse. Lei (2003) explains:

> By choosing to adopt markers associated with black masculinity, which has been stereotyped as hypermasculine and a threat to white male prerogative (Ferguson 2000), the Southeast Asian male students gained a tougher image. However, this tougher image also materialized them as deviant academic and social beings. (p. 177)

The number of boys at UHS who express a counterhegemonic masculinity is growing.

Houa is an example of a student who expressed the counterhegemonic masculinity at UHS. Identified by teachers and administrators as a chronic truant, Houa was difficult to track down. Teachers identified him as a student who was likely to be involved with gangs. I eventually met him one afternoon when I was interviewing another Hmong American male during study hall. As we neared the end of the interview, Houa walked into the cafeteria with a swagger that exaggerated the masculine conventions of body carriage held by mainstream society. Houa's clothes—baggy pants and oversized shirt and coat—are characterized by teachers and Hmong adults as "gang-type clothes." When I asked my interviewee about his plans for the future, Houa chimed in with "I'm going to be really rich. I'm going to have my own island named after me." When I asked Houa how he planned to make his money he asserted, "I'm going to own a big company, worldwide" and with that he walked away laughing.

After our initial meeting, I didn't see much of Houa again until the following year. I learned that Houa had failed to earn the requisite credits to be promoted and was being forced to repeat his ninth-grade year. He spent mornings at a newly created "school within a school" for students who had been retained, and then came back to UHS in the afternoons for a couple of classes. During his afternoon classes, Houa often put his head down on the desk, thereby raising the ire of his teachers. When I asked him about school, he simply stated, "School is boring." Like other chronic truants, Houa began skipping school because he was having problems keeping up with the work in his classes. Once he began skipping, however, his academic difficulties escalated.

One of Houa's teachers reported that although she had repeatedly encouraged Houa to come see her for extra help with his academic skills, he rarely did. She suggested that Houa was simply "too proud" to seek out help publicly. In my observations, I found that Americanized boys rarely approached teachers or other UHS educators for academic assistance or personal support. Their reluctance to go to teachers for help may be related to ideas regarding gender. Although I never heard any of the young men say that they were uncomfortable seeking help from female teachers, a few young Hmong women suggested that Hmong boys might be "too proud" to ask a woman for help. As mentioned earlier, within traditional Hmong culture men are seen as the ultimate authorities, and women are seen as subordinate (Donnelly, 1994; Rumbaut & Ima, 1988). Thus, it is reasonable to imagine that Houa and other Hmong American boys may avoid going to their female teachers for help because they do not recognize female authority. From this perspective, going to female teachers may actually be a threat to their expression of masculinity. Although Houa may be acting out traditional ideas regarding gender, his unwillingness to accept the authority of female teachers put him at odds with the school culture. By contrast, young men like Kao have positive relationships with their male and female teachers. Kao's ability to maintain positive relationships with female teachers is an example of the accommodation without assimilation associated with the new ideal Hmong American masculinity.

Although Houa dreams of being wealthy, education does not figure into his plans to achieve mobility. In fact, he does not have any clear ideas about how he might achieve his economic dreams. Inasmuch as education has been embraced as central to the Hmong American community's definition of ideal masculinity, Houa's rejection of school represents a rejection of the new ideal Hmong American masculinity. Houa's problems in school have led to repeated conflict with his parents. Houa and his friends routinely fight with their parents over issues like school, respect for elders, and clothing styles. Unlike Kao, who hopes that his individual success will benefit his family, Houa dreams of individual success. Houa and his friends dream of being "really rich" so they can own the consumer goods they covet. In particular, he dreams of having enough money to buy a nice/fast car.

Unlike Kao, who has been able to emulate aspects of the hegemonic masculinity of the school, Houa's academic difficulties prevent him from achieving a central quality associated with the school's hegemonic masculinity. In fact, Houa's academic difficulties and chronic truancy put him in direct opposition to the hegemonic masculinity of the school. Unable and unwilling to achieve masculinity through academic success, Houa has turned to other models of masculinity present at the school and in the popular culture. Specifically, Houa expresses a hypermasculinity. Houa and other chronic truants focus on a style of masculinity that emphasizes toughness, consumerism, and resistance to authority. Nice/fast cars, for example, are associated with dominant American expressions of masculine power. Their choice of clothes and their swaggering walks are also symbols of their hypermasculinity.

Again, it is important to stress that the school does not view the hypermasculinity expressed by Houa as a legitimate expression of masculinity. Hypermasculinity, in fact, is seen as dangerous and problematic. Not insignificantly, the hypermasculinity expressed by Houa and his friends is in direct contrast to the stereotype of Asian American men as weak, passive, and nonmasculine. Hypermasculinity is commonly associated with African American men, and as such young Hmong men who express hypermasculinity are blackened in the dominant imagination. UHS educators associate hypermasculinity with gang membership. Students who express this type of masculinity are characterized as having become "Americanized in a bad way." Adults in the Hmong American community also hold negative opinions about boys who express this form of masculinity. In short, Houa's expression of masculinity is in opposition to both the hegemonic masculinity of the school and the new ideal masculinity of the Hmong American community, which requires a level of accommodation to dominant norms without total assimilation.

CONCLUSION

In short, the Hmong American youth at UHS are negotiating new ways of expressing and performing their gendered identities in response to the multiple, complex, and often contradictory messages about gender they receive at home, school, and in the larger U.S. society. The Hmong American boys in my study are all struggling with how to be men in a larger society that tells them that they are not "real men" and not "real Americans." Their expressions of masculinity are responses to racialized and gendered inequalities at UHS and in the larger U.S. society. Because whiteness is central to the hegemonic masculinity of the school and larger society, it is impossible for any Hmong American boy to achieve hegemonic masculinity. Thus, Hmong American expressions of masculinity do not challenge the legitimacy of the hegemonic masculinity of the school.

Like Hmong American young men, most Hmong American young women see the United States as being dominated by Whites. Most Hmong American girls, however, assume that American culture offers greater gender equality for girls and women than Hmong culture. Traditional girls' beliefs about the opportunities for girls and women in the United States are often confirmed by their school experiences, where they encounter teachers invested in helping young women they perceive to be victims of a patriarchal culture.

The Hmong American youth at UHS demonstrate that the negotiation of various expressions of masculinity and femininity and the struggle over gender roles are central to the stories of immigrant students.

Race and the "Good" School

Like other first- and second-generation immigrant youth in the United States, the Hmong American high school students in my study were racialized through their school experiences and their encounters with the larger society. Their experiences demonstrate, in fact, that the process of racialization is central to the process of becoming American. Hmong American students at University Heights High School are surrounded by hegemonic messages about race. As in the larger society, Hmong American students confront the racial hierarchy that positions Whites at the top at UHS. Represented as the norm, whiteness is the standard against which all others are judged. As I argued throughout the book, for example, teachers' definitions of "good" and educable students reflect their assumptions regarding the normalcy of whiteness. Through their school experiences Hmong American students learn that whiteness and "normal" Americanness are constructed as one and the same.

As Asian Americans, Hmong American youth must also negotiate the racial stereotypes that cast Asian Americans as perpetual foreigners and/or model minorities. That mainstream teachers view Hmong American students, even those in mainstream classes, as the sole responsibility of the ESL program reflects the teachers' assumption regarding the essential "foreignness" of Hmong Americans. While East Asian American students at UHS are characterized as model minorities, most Hmong American students fail to achieve the levels of success equated with the model minority. Their inability to achieve model minority standards has led some teachers to view Hmong youth as culturally deficient.

High rates of poverty within the Hmong American community contributed to their exclusion from the model minority category, and have led to their ideological blackening (Ong, 1999, 2003). Many Hmong American youth have internalized a sense of shame about being poor, a fact that suggests that they have accepted the myth of meritocracy. Thus, the experiences of Hmong American youth at UHS demonstrate that class, as it intersects with race, shapes immigrant experiences as well.

Gender, as it intersects with race and class, also informs the immigrant experience. Gender shapes Hmong students' responses to school, and influences their perceptions of life in the United States. Hmong American girls, particularly those characterized as traditional, view schools as spaces that offer gender equality. Teachers' raced and classed assumptions regarding gender influence their responses to Hmong American students. Significantly, teachers' beliefs about the patriarchal nature of Hmong culture lead them to be more sympathetic toward Hmong American girls than boys.

Hmong American students form their identities in response to and within the context of the racial hegemony of UHS and the larger society. Their ideas about race, class, and gender are affected by what they observe and experience at UHS. Both traditional and Americanized students have internalized the idea that Whites are the only authentic Americans. For them, the term "American" is synonymous with White. Americanized youth recognize the stigma associated with foreignness, and they respond by distancing themselves from traditional Hmong youth and by dressing in hip-hop–style clothing in order to symbolize their Americanized identities.

Although race constrains the experiences and identities of Hmong American students at University Heights High, they are not simply passive victims of racism. Hmong youth respond in multiple and complex ways to the messages about race. While there is certainly evidence that many have internalized some racist messages, there is also evidence of resilience in the face of racial discrimination. Students in both the traditional and Americanized groups hid aspects of their culture that they assumed would be judged negatively by the dominant society. While it may seem as if hiding aspects of their culture reflects the internalization of the dominant norms, I would argue that the practice of hiding could also be viewed as a form of resistance. The practice of selective acculturation or accommodation without assimilation that was adopted by some traditional and some Americanized students reflects their understanding of the need to respond to unequal relations of power.

The oppositional attitude adopted by most Americanized students is, at least in part, a response to the racism of the school. For these students, hip-hop style holds oppositional power. Their style and attitude represent an inchoate critique of an educational system that excludes them. The fact that UHS staff view hip-hop style with suspicion reflects the staff's racial bias.

REVISITING THEORIES OF SEGMENTED ASSIMILATION

Recent research on immigrants highlights the importance of selective acculturation, defined as the preservation of aspects of the ethnic culture and the concomitant acquisition of aspects of the dominant culture, in the success of immigrant groups (Gibson, 1988; Portes & Rumbaut, 2001; Portes

& Zhou, 1993; Zhou & Bankston, 1998). From this perspective the maintenance of cultural traditions and social capital in the form of connections to the ethnic community can protect immigrant youth from the dangers of Americanization. According to this literature on segmented assimilation, the adoption of oppositional identities among immigrant youth is evidence of over-Americanization (Portes & Rumbaut, 2001; Portes & Zhou, 1993; Zhou, 1997; Zhou & Bankston, 1998). The assumption is that over-Americanized youth have lost their cultures, and are thus at risk for downward mobility.

Hmong American youth at University Heights High are all engaging in various forms of selective acculturation. My research confirms that parents and youth who engage in selective acculturation are more likely to experience positive intergenerational relations. Hmong American students who are connected to their cultures are better able to communicate with their parents. Culturally connected students also have a sense of pride in their identities that helps them persist in face of adversity. In short, my research reaffirms that immigrant groups must both preserve and transform their cultures in response to the racial and cultural context of the United States. As one Hmong American wrote in the first anthology of Hmong American writers, "The future of the Hmong should be what we are trying to create and not just what we are trying to preserve" (Cha, 2002, p. 33). Both traditional and Americanized youth are re-creating their cultures in response to contact with the dominant society.

Although there are clear benefits to selective acculturation, my research suggests that culture and social capital cannot entirely protect youth from racial inequality. While the literature on segmented assimilation focuses attention on the strength of immigrant communities, it underestimates the racial and economic barriers that low-income youth of color face. It fails to recognize that the formation of oppositional identities among immigrant youth represents a legitimate critique of the inequality that they face in schools and in the larger society.

My data also challenge the assumption that youth who have adopted oppositional identities have entirely assimilated and lost their ethnic cultures. Americanized males who express a counterhegemonic masculinity, for example, appear to hold some very traditional ideas regarding male superiority. All Americanized youth are attempting to re-create their culture and identities in response to conditions in the United States. Like other Asian American cultures, the Hmong American culture is hybrid in nature (Lowe, 1996). Americanized Hmong youth are attempting to create a new Hmong American culture that borrows, modifies, and transforms aspects of Hmong culture, dominant American culture, and various other American cultures.

MAKING "GOOD" SCHOOLS

Like other immigrant youth, the Hmong American students at University Heights High School learn lessons regarding race and their place in the racial hierarchy inside and outside of school. While schools are not solely responsible for the racial inequality that Hmong American students experience, and schools alone cannot solve the problems of racism, schools can work to challenge racism. The differences between the experiences of Americanized and traditional Hmong students suggest that schools can make a difference in the lives of immigrant youth. My data demonstrate that the success of many traditional students was due not only to their cultural connectedness, but also to the relatively supportive environment in the ESL program. My findings, however, should not be read as a blanket endorsement of ESL programs. As I argued in chapter 3, it is the culturally sensitive instruction offered by some of the teachers that is at the heart of many traditional students' success. Furthermore, my data show that the failure of UHS to accommodate the needs of Hmong American students in mainstream classes contributed to the formation of oppositional identities among Americanized students.

Americanized students' alienation from school raises significant questions regarding the characteristics of a good school. As noted throughout the book, University Heights High School has a reputation for academic excellence. In fact, according to many standard indicators, UHS is a good school. UHS faculty and staff are highly educated and experienced. The school offers a wide range of academic courses, and a wide range of extracurricular activities. The mean scores for UHS students on the SAT and ACT are higher than national averages. While UHS appears to be a good school for middle-class White students, it falls short of being a good school for most Hmong American youth, and other low-income students of color.

One of the most significant weaknesses of UHS is the relative absence of any meaningful multicultural education. As noted in chapter 3, many Americanized Hmong students are disconnected from the school's Eurocentric curriculum. Hmong American students crave a curriculum that includes their history and reflects their current experiences with inequality. In short, they want to see themselves in the official curriculum. Of course, these students need to be exposed to literatures and histories beyond their own, but they are right to critique a curriculum that completely denies their identities. A focus on Asian American history, specifically the history of Southeast Asian American refugees' arrival in the United States, would help Hmong American students understand their own history, and educate non-Hmong students about the relationship between Hmong history and U.S. history. By teaching the history of various ethnic and racial groups in the United States, particularly the history of Asian Americans, UHS could help to challenge the notion that Whites are the only real Americans. In addition to an examination of history, multicultural education should provide opportunities to examine the current experiences of various groups of color, including Hmong Americans.

I want to emphasize that I am advocating a multicultural education that focuses on critical accounts of inequality, as opposed to multicultural efforts that offer additive stories that leave the status quo unchallenged (Sleeter, 1996; Sleeter & Grant, 1987; Sleeter & McLaren, 1995). In other words, I would argue that multicultural efforts should include discussions of structural inequality. In addition to a focus on race, multicultural education should include discussions about the relationship between racism and other forms of social inequality.

Like others who advocate a critical multicultural education, I believe that it is imperative that students learn how to challenge inequality (Sleeter, 1996). Students need to understand how they can be active agents of change. Research suggests that most successful students of color are those who fully understand how racism functions, and view education as a way to resist racism (Lee, 1996; O'Connor, 1997). Although Americanized Hmong students are angry about the racism they experience, they are unable to connect their personal experiences with racism to larger structural issues. Furthermore, they do not know any constructive ways to confront racism. They do not see, for example, how academic achievement can be a form of resistance to racism.

My research also indicates that multicultural education should include a critical examination of whiteness. White students need the opportunity to reflect on their own racial privilege in order to challenge inequality (Lewis, 2001; Perry, 2002). White students also need opportunities to examine their own cultures in order to help them see the constructed nature of all cultures. In order to demonstrate the socially constructed nature of race, White students and students of color should be taught the history of how various European American groups became identified as White.

My study confirms previous research on the impact of popular culture on youth from immigrant families (Lee & Vaught, 2003; Olsen, 1997; Pyke, 2000). Although I was not initially interested in the influence of popular culture on Hmong American youth, I quickly learned that they glean information about "America" and "being American" from various forms of popular and consumer culture. Like other youth, Hmong American students spend hours each week watching TV, listening to popular music, and hanging out at local shopping malls. The Hmong American students at UHS gather information regarding Americans (read: Whites),

African Americans, social class, gender, and sexuality from TV. Schools cannot afford to ignore the influence of popular and consumer cultures on young people. Schools need to be actively involved in teaching students to become critical consumers of TV, popular music, movies, video games, magazines, and other forms of popular and consumer culture.

My data confirm the importance of trusting and caring relationships between students and teachers (Erickson, 1987; Ladson-Billings, 1995; Valenzuela, 1999). At UHS, Americanized youth who are disconnected from the faculty complain that teachers do not care about them as people. According to these students, "good" teachers need to know about the backgrounds, and lives of their students. While many ESL teachers at UHS are knowledgeable about immigrant students, many mainstream teachers know little about their Hmong American students. The work of educating students from immigrant backgrounds, however, should not be the sole responsibility of the ESL staff. All teachers who work with immigrant students need to know about the daily concerns facing immigrant families and communities. They need an understanding of how to work with immigrant communities to help children succeed in school. Teacher education programs should include education about immigrant youth and English-language learners (Goodwin, 2002; Valdes, 2001).

Schools that serve students from low-income immigrant families need to provide them with explicit information regarding the negotiation of high school and postsecondary schooling. Like other students from low-income families, the students in my study are largely unaware of the rules of the culture of power (Delpit, 1988). Many Americanized Hmong students, for example, do not have the requisite knowledge to make informed decisions regarding course selection. They also lack information regarding the requirements for college admissions. At UHS, information about postsecondary education is available in the guidance office and from members of the staff assigned to work with students of color. Many Hmong American students, however, are uncomfortable visiting the guidance office, and the opportunities offered by specialized staff provide only sporadic support. The students' experiences suggest that information about the culture of power needs to be integrated into the regular curriculum. Immigrant students need consistent and ongoing educational support.

Schools should also reach out to immigrant parents and do more to bring them into schools. Schools need to continue working to overcome language and cultural barriers which inhibit immigrant parent involvement. Immigrant parents must also be exposed to the rules of the culture of power. While I appreciate concerns regarding the ethnocentric nature of some parent education programs, I do not believe that efforts to inform parents about the American educational system are inherently problematic (Valdes, 1996). Parents new to the United States and unfamiliar with the American educational system need information about how schools operate, and how they can best support and advocate for their children. Of course, these efforts should be reciprocal, providing opportunities for immigrant parents to educate teachers and other staff about the immigrant culture. While parents must have chances to learn about the culture of American schools, they must also have opportunities to communicate to educators what they want from these institutions.

In addition to working towards better relationships with immigrant parents, schools need to make connections with immigrant community organizations. In many low-income immigrant neighborhoods, community organizations play a central role in supporting the education of youth. There are, for example, numerous Hmong American community organizations across the country that run educational programs and social support groups for Hmong youth. By building relationships with community organizations, schools can learn more about the lives of immigrant students. Moreover, relationships between schools and community organizations can support the work of each institution. As new Hmong refugees enter the United States, it will be important for schools to work with families and community organizations.

Finally, my research underscores the fact that faculty and staff need to recognize the way their identities influence their work with students. At UHS there were many well-meaning and dedicated White teachers who appeared to be largely unaware of the way race functioned at the school and in the larger society. They were, for example, unaware of the way race informed their definitions of "good" students. Their lack of awareness about race meant that they were unable to actively challenge racial inequality. It also meant that they were often unknowing perpetuators of racial inequality. UHS teachers, and most White educators, need opportunities to examine White privilege.

In summary, I have argued that University Heights High School largely reflects and reproduces the racial inequality of the larger society. These assumptions about race shape the educational experiences of all students, including youth from immigrant families. Schools, however, do not have to perpetuate racial inequality. In fact, schools can do much to challenge inequality. My research suggests that good schools must recognize the way race operates in the lives of students of color and White students. The experiences of Hmong American youth demonstrate that race matters in the United States. Good schools cannot ignore race, but must work to actively challenge racism.

References

Abu-Lughod, L. (1991). Writing against culture. In R. Fox (Ed.), *Recapturing anthropology: Working in the present* (pp. 137–162). Santa Fe, NM: School of American Research Press.

Appiah, A. (1996). Race, culture and identity—Misunderstood connections. In A. Appiah & A. Gutmann (Eds.), *Color conscious: The political morality of race* (pp. 30–105). Princeton: Princeton University Press.

Apple, M. (1993). *Official knowledge: Democratic education in a conservative age.* New York: Routledge Press.

Apple, M. (1996). *Cultural politics & education.* New York: Teachers College Press.

Associated Press. (2004, May 16). The arrival of 900 Hmong child refugees challenges Fresno schools. Napanews.com.

Au, K., & Mason, J. (1981). Social organizational factors in learning to read: The balance of rights hypothesis. *Reading Research Quarterly, 17*(1),115–152.

Balibar, E. (1992). Is there a "neo-racism"? In E. Balibar & I. Wallerstein (Eds.), *Race, nation, class: Ambiguous identities* (pp. 17–28). London: Verso.

Banks, J. A. (1995). Multicultural education: Historical development, dimensions, and practice. In J. A. Banks (Ed.), *Handbook of research on multicultural education* (pp. 3–24). New York: Macmillan.

Barney, G. L. (1957). *Christianity: Innovation in Meo culture.* Unpublished master's thesis, University of Minnesota.

Barth, F. (Ed.). (1969). *Ethnic groups and boundaries: The social organization of culture difference.* Boston: Little, Brown.

Beck, R. (1994, April). The ordeal of immigration in Wausau. *Atlantic Monthly,* pp. 84–97.

Bell, D. (1992). *Faces at the bottom of the well: The permanence of racism.* New York: Basic Books.

Bennett, C. I. (1999). *Comprehensive multicultural education: Theory and practice (4th ed.).* Boston: Allyn & Bacon.

Bourdieu, P. (1984). *Distinction: A social critique of the judgment of taste.* Cambridge, MA: Harvard University Press.

Cammarto, J. (2004). The gendered and racialized pathways of Latina and Latino youth: Different struggles, different resistances in the urban context. *Anthropology & Education Quarterly, 35*(1), 53–74.

Cha, B. (2002). Being Hmong is not enough. In M. Moua (Ed.), *Bamboo among the oaks: Contemporary writing by Hmong Americans*. St. Paul: Minnesota Historical Society Press.

Chan, S. (1991). *Asian American: An interpretive history*. Boston: Twayne Publishers.

Cheung, K. (1993). *Articulate silences: Hisaye Yamamoto, Maxine Hong Kingston, Joy Kogawa*. Ithaca, NY: Cornell University Press.

Clifford, J., & Marcus, G. E. (1986). *Writing culture: The poetics and politics of ethnography*. Berkeley: University of California Press.

Cohn, M. (1986). Hmong youth and Hmong culture in America. In G. Hendricks, B. Downing, & A. Deinard (Eds.), *The Hmong in transition* (pp. 197–201). Staten Island, NY: Center for Migration Studies.

Collins, P. H. (2000). *Black feminist thought: Knowledge, consciousness, and the politics of empowerment (2nd ed.)*. New York: Routledge.

Comer, J. P. (1980). *School power*. New York: Free Press.

Connell, R. W. (1993). Disruptions: Improper masculinities and schooling. In L. Weis & M. Fine (Eds.), *Beyond silenced voices: Class, gender and race in U.S. schools* (pp. 191–208). Albany: State University of New York Press.

Connell, R. W. (1995). *Masculinities*. Berkeley: University of California Press.

Crenshaw, K., et al. (Eds.). (1995). *Critical race theory: The key writings that formed the movement*. New York: New Press.

Cummins, J. (1986). Empowering minority students: A framework for intervention. *Harvard Educational Review, 56*(1), 18–36.

Dance, L. J. (2002). *Tough fronts: The impact of street culture on schooling*. New York: Routledge Falmer.

Delpit, L. (1988). The silenced dialogue: Power and pedagogy in educating other people's children. *Harvard Educational Review, 58*(3), 280–298.

Doerfler, J. (2001). *Parents in school decision making: Some unanticipated consequences*. Unpublished master's thesis, University of Wisconsin-Madison.

Donnelly, N. (1994). *Changing lives of refugee Hmong women*. Seattle: University of Washington Press.

Dunnigan, T. (1986). Processes of identity maintenance in Hmong society. In G. Hendricks, B. Downing, & A. Deinard (Eds.), *The Hmong in transition* (pp. 41–53). Staten Island, NY: Center of Migration Studies.

Dyer, R. (1993). *The matter of images: Essays on representations*. New York: Routledge.

Eckert, P. (1989). *Jocks and burnouts: Social categories and identity in the high school*. New York: Teachers College Press.

Epstein, J. L. (1992). School and family partnerships. In M. Alkin (Ed.), *Encyclopedia of Educational Research* (6th ed.) (pp. 1139–1151). New York: Macmillan.

Epstein, J. L. (1995). School/family/community partnerships: Caring for the children we share. *Phi Delta Kappan*, 701–712.

Erickson, F. (1986). Qualitative methods. In R. Linn & F. Erickson (Eds.), *Research in teaching and learning: Quantitative methods, qualitative methods*. New York: MacMillan.

Erickson, F. (1987). Transformation and School Success: The politics and culture of educational achievement. *Anthropology & Education Quarterly, 18*(4), 335–356.

Erickson, F., & Mohatt, G. (1982). Cultural organization of participation structures in two classrooms of Indian students. In G. Spindler (Ed.), *Doing the ethnography of schooling: Educational anthropology in action* (pp. 132–175). New York: Holt, Rinehart & Winston.

Espiritu, Y. (1992). *Asian American panethnicity: Bridging institutions and identities.* Philadelphia: Temple University Press.

Espiritu, Y. (2000). *Asian American women and men.* Walnut Creek, CA: Altamira Press.

Faderman, L., & Xiong, G. (1998). *I begin my life all over: The Hmong and the American immigrant experience.* Boston: Beacon Press.

Fadimann, A. (1997). *The spirit catches you and you fall down: A Hmong child, her American doctors, and the collision of two cultures.* New York: Farrar, Straus and Giroux.

Fass, S. (1991). *The Hmong in Wisconsin: On the road to self-sufficiency.* Milwaukee: Wisconsin Policy Research Institute.

Feagin, J. (2000). *Racist America: Roots, current realities and future reparations.* New York: Routledge.

Ferguson, A. (2000). *Bad boys: Public schools in the making of black masculinity.* Ann Arbor: University of Michigan Press.

Fine, M. (1991). *Framing dropouts: Notes on the politics of an urban public high school.* Albany: State University of New York Press.

Fine, M. (1993). [Ap]parent involvement: Reflections on parents, power, and urban public schools. *Teachers College Record, 94,* 682–710.

Fine, M. (1994). Working the hyphens: Reinventing self and other in qualitative research. In N. R. Denzin & Y. S. Lincoln (Eds.), *Handbook of qualitative research* (pp. 70–82). Thousand Oaks, CA: Sage.

Fine, M., & Weis, L. (1998). *The unknown city: The lives of poor and working class young adults.* Boston: Beacon.

Fish, A. (1991). *The Hmong of St. Paul, Minnesota: The effects of culture, gender, and the family networks on adolescents' plans for the future.* Unpublished master's thesis, University of Minnesota.

Fiske, J. (1994). *Media matters: Everyday culture and political change.* Minneapolis: University of Minnesota Press.

Foley, D. (1990). *Learning capitalist future: Deep in the heart of Tejas.* Philadelphia: University of Pennsylvania Press.

Fordham, S. (1996). *Blacked out: Dilemmas of race, identity, and success at Capital High.* Chicago: University of Chicago Press.

Fordham, S., & Ogbu, J. U. (1986). Black students' school success: Coping with the "burden of 'acting white.'" *Urban Review 18*(3), 176–206.

Frankenberg, R. (1993). *White women, race matters: The social construction of whiteness.* Minneapolis: University of Minnesota Press.

Frankenberg, R. (2001). The mirage of unmarked whiteness. In B. Rasmussen, E. Klinenberg, I. Nexica, & M. Wray (Eds.), *The making and unmaking of whiteness* (pp. 72–96). Durham, NC: Duke University Press.

Gallagher, C. A. (2000). White like me? Methods, meaning, and manipulation in the field of white studies. In T. Winddace & J. W. Warren (Eds.), *Racing research researching race.* New York: New York University Press.

Gans, H. (1992). Second generation decline: Scenarios for the economic and ethnic futures of the post-1965 American immigrants. *Ethnic and Racial Studies, 15,* 173–192.

Gibson, M. (1988). *Accommodation without assimilation: Sikh immigrants in an American high school.* Ithaca, NY: Cornell University Press.

Gillespie, M. A. (1998). Mirror, mirror. In R. Weitz (Ed.), *The politics of women's bodies: Sexuality, appearance, and behavior* (pp. 184–188). New York: Oxford.

Gilroy, P. (1990). One nation under groove: The cultural politics of "race" and racism in Britain. In D. T. Goldberg (Ed.), *Anatomy of racism* (pp. 263–282). Minneapolis: University of Minnesota Press.

Gitlin, A., Buendia, E., Crosland, K., & Doumbia, F. (2003). The production of margin and center: Welcoming-unwelcoming immigrant students. *American Educational Research Journal, 40*(1), 91–122.

Goldstein, B. (1985). *Schooling for cultural transitions: Hmong girls & boys in American high schools.* Unpublished doctoral dissertation, University of Wisconsin-Madison.

Goldstein, B. (1986). Resolving sexual assault: Hmong and the American legal system. In G. Hendricks, B. Downing, & A. Deinard (Eds.), *The Hmong in transition* (pp. 135–143). Staten Island, New York: Center for Migration Studies.

Goodwin, A. L. (2002). Teacher education and the education of immigrant children. *Education in Urban Society, 34*(2), 156–172.

Gordon, M. M. (1964). *Assimilation in American life: The role of race, religion, and national origins.* New York: Oxford University Press.

Gotanda, N. (1995). A critique of "Our Constitution Is Color-Blind." In K. Crenshaw, N. Gotanda, G. Peller, & K. Thomas (Eds.), *Critical race theory: The key writings that formed the movement* (pp. 257–275). New York: The New Press.

Greenhouse, S. (2003, July 13). Going for the look, but risking discrimination. *New York Times,* p. 10.

Guinier, L., & Torres, G. (2002). *The miner's canary: Enlisting race, resisting power, transforming democracy.* Cambridge, MA: Harvard University Press.

Hall, S. (1996). The question of cultural identity. In S. Hall, D. Held, D. Hubert, & K. Thompson (Eds.), *Modernity: An introduction to modern societies.* Oxford: Blackwell.

Hall, K. (2002). *Lives in translation: Sikh youth as British citizens.* Philadelphia: University of Pennsylvania Press.

Heath, S. B. (1983). *Ways with words: Language, life, and work in communities and classrooms.* Cambridge, England: Cambridge University Press.

Hein, J. (1994). From migrant to minority: Hmong refugees and the social construction of identity in the United States. *Sociological Inquiry, 64*(3), 281–306.

Hein, J. (1996, Spring). Wisconsin's Hmong leaders. *Kaleidoscope II,* University of Wisconsin System Institute on Race and Ethnicity, pp. 3–8.

Hendricks, G. (1986). Introduction. In G. Hendricks, B. Downing, & A. Deinard (Eds.), *The Hmong in transition* (pp. 3–5). New York: Center for Migration Studies.

Hess, R., & Shipman, V. (1965). Early experience and the socialization of cognitive modes in children. *Child Development, 36,* 869–876.

Ho, J. (2004). *I think I'm turning Japanese? R. Kelly, Keanu Reaves, and passing through Asian America.* Paper presented at 2004 Association of Asian American Studies Conference, Boston, MA.

Hobbel, N. (2003). *Imagining the good teacher.* Unpublished doctoral dissertation, University of Wisconsin, Madison.

Holland, D., & Eisenhart, M. (1991). *Educated in romance: Women, achievement, and college culture.* Chicago: University of Chicago Press.

Hurtado, A., & Stewart, A. (1997). Through the looking glass: Studying whiteness for feminist methods. In M. Fine, L. Weis, L. Powell, & L. M. Wong (Eds), *Off White: Readings on race, power and society* (pp. 57–65). New York: Routledge.

Hutchinson, R. (1992). *Acculturation in the Hmong community.* Green Bay: Center for Public Affairs, University of Wisconsin; Milwaukee: Institute on Race and Ethnicity, University of Wisconsin.

Ignatiev, N. (1995). *How the Irish became white.* New York: Routledge.

Islam, N. (2000). Research as an act of betrayal: Researching race in an Asian community in Los Angeles. In F. W Twine & J. W. Warren (Eds.), *Racing research researching race.* New York: New York University Press.

Jaret, C. (1999). Troubles by newcomers: Anti-immigrant attitudes and action during two eras of mass immigration to the United States. *Journal of American Ethnic History, 18*(3), 9–39.

Kailin, J. (1999). How White teachers perceive the problem of racism in their schools: A case study in "liberal" Lakeview. *Teachers College Record, 100*(4), 724–750.

Kao, G., & Tienda, M. (1995). Optimism and achievement: The educational performance of immigrant youth. *Social Science Quarterly, 76,* 1–19.

Kelley, R. (1997). *Yo' mama's disFunktional: Fighting the culture wars in urban America.* New York: Beacon Press.

Kenny, L. (2000). *Daughters of suburbia: Growing up white, middle class and female.* New Brunswick, NJ: Rutgers University Press.

Kibria, N. (1993). *Family tightrope: The changing lives of Vietnamese Americans.* Princeton, NJ: Princeton University Press.

Kimmel, M. (1994). Masculinity as homophobia. In H. Brod & M. Kaufman (Eds.), *Theorizing masculinities* (pp. 119–141). Thousand Oaks, CA: Sage.

Kimmel, M (2000). Introduction. In M. Kimmel & A. Aronson (Eds.), *The gendered society reader* (pp. 1–6). New York: Oxford University Press.

Kincheloe, J. L., Steinberg, S. R., Rodriquez, N. M., & Chennault, R. E. (Eds.). (1991). *White reign: Deploying whiteness in America.* New York: St. Martin's.

King, J. (1991). Dysconscious racism: Ideology, identity, and the miseducation of teachers. *Journal of Negro Education, 60*(2), 133–146.

Koltyk, J. (1998). *New pioneers in the heartland: Hmong life in Wisconsin.* Boston: Allyn & Bacon.

Koza, J. E. (1994). Rap music: The cultural politics of official representation. *The Review of Education/Pedagogy/Cultural Studies, 16*(2), 171–196.

Kumashiro, K. (1998). Reading queer Asian American masculinities and sexualities in elementary school. In J. Sears & W. Letts (Eds.), *Teaching queerly:*

Affirming diversity in elementary school (pp. 61–70). Lanham, MD: Rowman & Littlefield.

Kurien, P. (1999). Gendered ethnicity: Creating a Hindu Indian identity in the United States. *American Behavioral Scientist, 42*(4), 648–670.

Ladson-Billings, G. (1995). Toward a culturally relevant pedagogy. *American Educational Research Journal, 32,* 465–491.

Lareau, A. (2000). *Home advantage: Social class and parental intervention in elementary education.* Lanham, MD: Rowman & Littlefield.

Lee, G. (1996). Cultural identity in a postmodern society: Reflections on what is Hmong? *Hmong Studies Journal, 1*(1), http://members.aol.com/hmongstudies/HSJ.html.

Lee, R. (1999). *Orientals: Asian Americans in popular culture.* Philadelphia: Temple University Press.

Lee, S. J. (1996). *Unraveling the model minority stereotype: Listening to Asian American youth.* New York: Teachers College Press.

Lee, S. J. (1997). The road to college: Hmong American women's pursuit of higher education. *Harvard Educational Review, 67*(4), 803–827.

Lee, S. J. (2001a). Transforming and exploring the landscape of gender and sexuality: Hmong American teenaged girls. *Race, Gender & Class, 8*(2), 35–46.

Lee, S. J. (2001b). More than "model minorities" or "delinquents": A look at Hmong American high school students. *Harvard Educational Review, 71*(3), 505–528.

Lee, S. J. (2004). Hmong American masculinities: Creating new identities in the United States. In N. Way & J. Chu (Eds.), A*dolescent boys: Exploring diverse cultures of boyhood.* New York: New York University Press.

Lee, S. J., & Vaught, S. (2003). "You can never be too rich or too thin": Popular and consumer culture and the Americanization of Asian American girls and young women. *Journal of Negro Education, 72*(4), 457–466.

Lefkowitz, B. (1997). *Our guys.* New York: Vintage Books.

Lei, J. (2001). *Claims to belonging and difference: Cultural citizenship and identity construction in schools.* Unpublished doctoral dissertation, University of Wisconsin-Madison.

Lei, J. (2003). (Un)necessary toughness?: Those "loud black girls" and those "quiet Asian boys." *Anthropology & Education Quarterly, 34*(2), 158–181.

Lewis, A. (2001). There is no "race" in the schoolyard: Color-blind ideology in an (almost) all-white school. *American Educational Research Journal, 38*(4), 781–811.

Lewis, O. (1966). The culture of poverty. *Scientific American, 215,* 19–25.

Lipman, P. (1998). *Race, class, and power in school restructuring.* Albany: State University of New York Press.

Loewen, J. (1971). *The Mississippi Chinese: Between black and white.* Cambridge, MA: Harvard University Press.

Lopez, N. (2003). *Hopeful girls, troubled boys: Race and gender disparity in urban education.* New York: Routledge.

Loutzenheiser, L. (2001). *Painting outside the lines? Tensions and possibilities of alter-*

native schools for marginalized students. Unpublished doctoral dissertation, University of Wisconsin-Madison.

Lowe, L. (1996). *Immigrant acts: On Asian American cultural politics.* Durham, NC: Duke University Press.

Lynch, A. (1999). *Dress, gender and cultural change: Asian American and African American rites of passage.* New York: Berg.

Marcus, G. (1995). *Ethnography through thick & thin.* Princeton, NJ: Princeton University Press.

Matute-Bianchi, M. (1986). Ethnic identities and patterns of school success and failure among Mexican-descent and Japanese American students in a California high school: An ethnographic analysis. *American Journal of Education, 95,* 233–255.

McIntosh, P. (1989, July/August). White privilege: Unpacking the invisible knapsack. *Peace and Freedom,* 10–12.

McLaren, P. (1998). Whiteness is . . . The struggle for postcolonial hybridity. In J. Kincheloe, S. Steinberg, N. Rodriguez, & R. Chennault (Eds.), *White reign: Deploying whiteness in America.* New York: St Martin's.

Metz, M. (1986). *Different by design: The context and character of three magnet schools.* New York: Routledge & Kegan Paul.

Moua, M. A. (Ed.). (2002). *Bamboo among the oaks: Contemporary writing by Hmong Americans.* St. Paul, Minnesota: Minnesota Historical Society Press.

Mydans, S. (2004, August 8). Indochina War refugees find homes at last in U.S. *New York Times,* p. 4.

Nakayama, T. (1994). Show/down time: Race, gender, sexuality and popular. *Critical Studies in Mass Communication, 11,* 162–179.

Ngo, B. (2000). *Obstacles, miracles and the pursuit of higher education: The experiences of Hmong American college students.* Unpublished master's thesis, University of Wisconsin-Madison.

Ngo, B. (2002). Contesting "culture": The perspectives of Hmong American female students on early marriage. *Anthropology and Education Quarterly, 33*(2), 163–188.

Nieto, S. (2000). *Affirming diversity: The sociopolitical context of multicultural education* (3rd ed.). New York: Longman.

Oakes, J. (1985). *Keeping track: How schools structure inequality.* New Haven, CT: Yale University Press.

O'Connor, C. (1997). Dispositions toward (collective) struggle and educational resilience in the inner city: A case analysis of six African American high school students. *American Educational Research Journal, 34*(4), 593–629.

Ogbu, J. (1987). Variability in minority school performance: A problem in search of an explanation. *Anthropology & Education Quarterly, 18*(4), 312–334.

Ogbu, J. (1992). Adaptation to minority status and impact on school success. *Theory into Practice, (31)*4, 287–295.

Okihiro, G. (1994). *Margins and mainstreams: Asians in American history and culture.* Seattle: University of Washington Press.

Olneck, M. (2004). Immigrants and education in the United States. In J. A. Banks

& C. A. M. Banks (Eds.), *Handbook of research on multicultural education* (pp. 381–403). New York: Macmillan.

Olsen, L. (1997). *Made in America: Immigrant students in our public schools.* New York: New Press.

Omi, M., & Winant, H. (1986). *Racial formation in the United States: From the 1960's to the 1990's.* New York: Routledge.

Omi, M., & Winant, H. (1994). *Racial formation in the United States: From the 1960's to the 1990's* (2nd ed.). New York: Routledge.

Ong, A. (1999). Cultural citizenship as subject making: Immigrants negotiate racial and cultural boundaries in the United States. In R. Torres, L. Miron, & J. Inda (Eds.), *Race, identity, and citizenship: A reader* (pp. 262–293). Malden, MA: Blackwell Publishing.

Ong, A. (2003). *Buddha is hiding: Refugees, citizenship, the new America.* Berkeley: University of California Press.

Orenstein, P. (1994). *School girls: Young women, self-esteem, and the confidence gap.* New York: Doubleday Anchor Books.

Osajima, K. (1991). Breaking the silence: Race and the educational experiences of Asian American college students. In M. Foster (Ed.), *Readings on equal education, volume 11: Qualitative investigations into schools and schooling.* New York: AMS Press.

Osajima, K. (1988). Asian Americans as the model minority: An analysis of the popular press image in the 1960's and 1980's. In G. Okihiro, S. Hune, A. Hansen, & J. Liu (Eds.), *Reflections on shattered windows: Promises and prospects for Asian American studies* (pp. 165–174). Pullman: Washington State University Press.

Page, R. N. (1991). *Lower-track classrooms: A curricular and cultural perspective.* New York: Teachers College Press.

Park, K. (1997). *The Korean American dream: Immigrants and small business in New York City.* Ithaca, NY: Cornell University Press.

Park, R. (1950). *Race and culture.* New York: Free Press.

Pascoe, P. (1990). *Relations of rescue: The search for female moral authority in the American west, 1874–1939.* New York and Oxford: Oxford University Press.

Perry, P. (2001). White means never having to say you are ethnic. *Journal of Contemporary Ethnography, 30*(1), 56–92.

Perry, P. (2002). *Shades of white: White kids and racial identities in high school.* Durham, NC: Duke University Press.

Pfeifer, M., & Lee, S. (2004). Hmong population, demographic, socioeconomic, and educational trends in the 2000 census. In Hmong National Development Inc. & Hmong Cultural and Resource Center (Eds.), *Hmong 2000 census publication: Data & analysis* (pp. 3–11). Washington, DC: Hmong National Development, Inc.

Philips, S. (1982). *The invisible culture: Communication in classroom and community on the Warm Springs Indian reservation.* New York: Longman.

Portes, A., (1996). *The new second generation.* New York: Russell Sage Foundation.

Portes, A., & Rumbaut, R. (1996). *Immigrant America: A portrait* (2nd ed.). Berkeley: University of California Press.

Portes, A., & Rumbaut, R. (2001). Conclusion: The forging of a New America: lessons for theory and policy. In R. Rumbaut & A. Portes (Eds.), *Ethnicities: Children of immigrants in America*. Berkeley: University of California Press.

Portes, A., & Rumbaut, R. (2001). *Legacies: The story of the immigrant second generation*. Berkeley: University of California Press.

Portes, A., & Zhou, M. (1993). *The new second generation: Segmented assimilation and its variants. Annals of the American Academy of Political and Social Sciences, 530*, 219–230.

Proweller, A. (1998). *Constructing female identities: Meaning making in an upper middle class youth culture*. Albany: State University of New York Press.

Pyke, K. (2000). The normal American family as an interpretive structure of family life among grown children of Korean and Vietnamese immigrants. *Journal of Marriage and the Family, 62*, 240–255.

Rains, F. (1998). Is the benign really harmless? Deconstructing some "benign" manifestations of operationalized white privilege. In J. Kincheloe, S. Steinberg, N. Rodriguez, & R. Chennault (Eds), *White reign: Deploying whiteness in America* (pp. 77–102). New York: St Martin's.

Roediger, D. (1991). *Wages of whiteness: Race and the making of the American working class*. New York: Verso.

Rong, X. L., & Preissle, J. (1997). The continuing decline in Asian American teachers. *American Educational Research Journal, 71*(3), 536–565.

Ruiz, R. (1984). Orientations in language planning. *NABE Journal, 8*(2), 15–38.

Rumbaut, R. (1991). The agony of exile: A study of Indochinese refugee adults and children. In F. L. Ahearn Jr. & J. L. Athey (Eds.), *Refugee children: Theory, research, and services*. Baltimore: Johns Hopkins University Press.

Rumbaut, R., & Ima, K. (1988). *The adaptation of Southeast Asian refugee youth: A comparative study*. Washington, DC: Office of Refugee Resettlement.

Scott, G. (1982). The Hmong refugee community in San Diego: Theoretical and practical implications of its continuing ethnic solidarity. *Anthropological Quarterly, 55*, 146–160.

Scott, G. (1988). To catch or not to catch a thief: A case of bride theft among the Lao Hmong refugees of Southern California. *Ethnic Groups, 7*, 137–151.

Sherman, S. (1988). The Hmong: Laotian refugees in the "land of the giants." *National Geographic, 174*, 586–610.

Sleeter, C. (1993). How white teachers construct race. In C. McCarthy & W. Chrichlow (Eds.), *Race, identity, & representation in education* (pp. 157–171). New York: Routledge.

Sleeter, C. (1996). *Multicultural education as social activism*. Albany: State University of New York Press.

Sleeter, C., & Grant, C. A. (1987). An analysis of multicultural education in the United States. *Harvard Educational Review, 57*(2), 421–444.

Sleeter, C., & Grant, C. A. (1999). *Making choices for multicultural education: Five approaches to race, class, and gender* (3rd ed.). New York: John Wiley & Sons.

Sleeter, C., & McLaren, P. (1995). *Multicultural education, critical pedagogy, and the politics of difference*. Albany: State University of New York Press.

Smith, L. (1999). *Decolonizing methodologies: Research and indigenous peoples*. London: Zed Books.

Smith-Hefner, N. J. (1999). *Kmer American: Identity and moral education in a diasporic community*. Berkeley: University of California Press.

Snyder, T. D., & Hoffman, C. M. (1994). *Digest of education statistics*. Report prepared for the National Center of Education Statistics, Washington, DC. (ERIC Document Reproduction Service No. ED377253).

Song, M. (1999). *Helping out: Children's labor in ethnic businesses*. Philadelphia: Temple University Press.

Sontag, D. (2003, November 16). In a homeland far from home. *New York Times Magazine*.

Stacey, J. (1988). Can there be a feminist ethnography? *Women's Studies International Forum, 11*(1), 21–27.

Stanton-Salazar, R. (2001). *Manufacturing hope and despair: The school and kin support networks of U.S.-Mexican youth*. New York: Teachers College Press.

Suarez-Orozco, M. (1989). *Central American refugees and U.S. high schools: A psychosocial study of motivation and achievement*. Stanford, CA: Stanford University Press.

Suarez-Orozco, M., & Suarez-Orozco, C. (2001). *Children of immigrants*. Cambridge, MA: Harvard University Press.

Suarez-Orozco, M., & Sung, B. (1987). *The adjustment experience of Chinese immigrant children in New York City*. Staten Island, New York: Center for Migration Studies.

Takagi, D. Y. (1992). *The retreat from race: Asian-American admissions and racial politics*. New Brunswick, NJ: Rutgers University Press.

Takaki, R. (1989). *Strangers from a different shore: A history of Asian Americans*. New York: Penguin.

Thao, P. (1999). *Hmong education at the crossroads*. New York: University Press of America.

Thorne, B. (1993). *Gender play: Girls and boys in school*. Rutgers, NJ: Rutgers University Press.

Tillman, L. (2002). Culturally sensitive research approaches: An African American perspective. *Educational Researcher, 31*(9), 3–12.

Tse, L. (2001). *"Why don't they learn English?": Separating fact from fallacy in the U.S. language debate*. New York: Teachers College Press.

Tsing, A. L. (1993). *In the realm of the diamond queen*. Princeton, NJ: Princeton University Press.

Tuan, M. (1998). *Forever foreigners or honorary whites?: The Asian ethnic experience today*. New Brunswick, NJ: Rutgers University Press.

Twine, F. (2000). Racial ideologies and racial methodologies. In F. Twine & J. Warren (Eds.), *Racing research, researching race* (pp. 1–33). New York: New York University Press.

U.S. Census Bureau. (2000a). (Summary File 1 [SF 1]. QT-P7.) Race alone or in combination for American Indian, Alaska native, and for selected categories of Asian and of Native Hawaiian and other Pacific islander. At http://factfinder.census.gov/

U.S. Census Bureau. (2000b). (Summary File 4 [SF-4]. QT-P35.) Poverty status in 1999 of families and nonfamily householders. At http://factfinder.census.gov/

U.S. Census Bureau. (2000c). (Summary File 4. QT-P20.) Educational attainment by sex. At http://factfinder.census.gov/

Valdes, G. (1996). *Con respeto: Bridging the distances between culturally diverse families and schools—an ethnographic portrait.* New York: Teachers College Press.

Valdes, G. (2001). *Learning and not learning English: Latino students in American schools.* New York: Teachers College Press.

Valenzuela, A. (1999). *Subtractive schooling: U.S.–Mexican youth and the politics of caring.* Albany: State University of New York Press.

Vang, C. (2004). Contested growth among Hmong Americans. In Hmong National Development Inc. & Hmong Cultural and Resource Center (Eds.), *Hmong 2000 Census Publication: Data & Analysis* (pp. 29–31). Washington, DC: Hmong National Development, Inc.

Vang, H. (2004). Hmong American women's educational attainment: Implications for Hmong American women and men. In Hmong National Development Inc. & Hmong Cultural and Resource Center (Eds.), *Hmong 2000 census publication: data & analysis* (pp. 23–25). Washington, DC: Hmong National Development, Inc.

Vang, K. (1982). Hmong marriage customs: A current assessment. In B. Downing & D. Olney (Eds.), *The Hmong in the West: Observations and Reports, Papers of the 1981 Hmong Research Conference at the University of Minnesota.* Southeast Asian Refugee Studies Project & Center for Urban and Regional Affairs, Minneapolis: University of Minnesota.

Verma, R. (2004). *Migration and memory: Reflections on schooling and community by Sikh immigrant youth.* Doctoral dissertation, University of Wisconsin-Madison.

Vo, L., & Danico, M. (2004). No lattes here: Asian American youth and the cyber café obsession. In M. Zhou & J. Lee (Eds.), *Asian American youth: Culture, identity and ethnicity* (in press). New York: Routledge.

Waldinger, R. (Ed.). (2001). *Strangers at the gate: New immigrants in urban America.* Berkeley: University of California Press.

Walker-Moffat, W. (1995). *The other side of the Asian American success story.* San Francisco: Jossey Bass.

Waters, M. (1990). *Ethnic options: Choosing identities in America.* Berkeley: University of California Press.

Waters, M. (1999). *Black identities: West Indian immigrant dreams and American realities.* Cambridge, MA: Harvard University Press.

Weiler, K. (1988). *Women teaching for change: Gender, class and power.* South Hadley, MA: Bergin & Garvey.

Weis, L., & Centrie, C. (2002). On the power of separate spaces: Teachers and students writing (righting) selves and future. *American Educational Research Journal, 39*(1), 7–36.

Willis, P. (1977). *Learning to labor: How working class kids get working class jobs.* New York: Columbia University Press.

Winant, H. (2001). *The world is a ghetto: race and democracy since World War II.* New York: Basic Books.

Wisconsin State Journal. (2004, January 25). *Thousands of Hmong must choose a home,*
p. D5.

Wu, F. H. (2002). *Yellow: Race in America beyond black and white.* New York: Basic
Books.

Yang, K., & Pfeifer, M. (2004). Profile of Hmong educational attainment. In Hmong
National Development Inc. & Hmong Cultural and Resource Center (Eds.),
Hmong 2000 census publication: Data & analysis (pp. 21–22). Washington, DC:
Hmong National Development, Inc.

Zhou, M. (1997). Growing up American: The challenge confronting immigrant
children and children of immigrants. *Annual Review of Sociology, 23,* 63–95.

Zhou, M. (2001). Straddling different worlds: The acculturation of Vietnamese
refugee children. In R. G. Rumbaut & A. Portes (Eds.), *Children of immigrants
in America.* New York: Russell Sage Foundation.

Zhou, M., & Bankston, C. (1998). *Growing up American: The adaptation of Vietnamese adolescents in the United States.* New York: Russell Sage Foundation.

Index

Abu-Lughod, L., 20
Academic achievement, 28, 52, 127
  of "Americanized" youth, 72–73, 74–79,
    103, 114, 115, 118, 119–20
  and becoming racialized Americans, 2,
    10, 11
  and cultural deficiency/deprivation, 48
  and gender issues, 90, 100–101, 102,
    103, 114, 115, 118, 119–20
  and "good" and "talented," 29–30, 50
  and interpretations of Hmong American
    students' experiences, 41–49
  and privileging "good" parents, 36, 38,
    40–41
  and reproducing racial hierarchy, 32–33
  and reputation of UHS, 25–26
  and "Traditional" youth, 52, 57, 60, 64,
    100–101, 102
Accommodation, 10, 19, 51, 84, 120, 121,
  124
Acculturation, 9, 10, 50–51, 63–64, 82,
  83–84, 102–3, 107, 124–25
"Acting White," 75
Administrators/staff, 3, 20
  and "Americanized" youth, 73, 115
  and gender issues, 90, 92, 93, 115
  and making "good" schools, 128, 129
  and race, 32–33, 124, 129
  role in reproduction of culture of, 26–
    28
African Americans, 18, 24, 38, 80
  and "Americanized" youth, 68–69, 79,
    103, 115, 119, 121
  as "bad," 4, 5, 46
  and becoming racialized Americans, 3–
    4, 6, 7
  characterizations of, 14
  and cultural deficiencies/differences,
    43, 45–46, 47, 48
  and gender issues, 92, 95, 99, 103, 115,
    119, 121
  and hip-hop culture, 69–70
  and oppositional identity of Whites, 70
  prejudice toward, 62
  and relationship between "Traditional"
    and "Americanized" youth, 55
  and reproducing racial hierarchy, 32,
    33
  and role of faculty and staff in
    reproduction of culture, 27–28
  and socioeconomic class, 68–69
  stereotyping of, 66, 119
  and "Traditional" youth, 61–62
  and White-Black dichotomy, 3–4, 5, 6,
    7
American-ness
  and cultural difference/deficiencies, 44,
    49
  Hmong views about, 49
  immigrants as threat to, 7, 14
  whiteness as central to, 4, 8, 35, 49,
    123
  Whites as authentic, 49, 55, 124, 127
  See also "Americanization"
"Americanization," 22, 72, 123
  as "bad," 6, 7, 9, 64, 107–12, 116, 118–
    21, 125
  characteristics of, 50–51
  as function of schools, 8
  and gender issues, 114–18
  as "good," 6–7, 51, 103–7, 114–18
  Hmong parents' views about, 50–51
  over-, 125
  See also Assimilation

143

"Americanized" youth
  academic achievement of, 72–73, 75–79
  "acting White" by, 75
  and African Americans, 68–69, 79
  alienation of, 77, 84, 110, 126
  aspirations of, 81–82, 104, 112, 114,
    118, 119, 120
  as "bad," 50, 69, 73, 82–84, 103, 107–
    12, 118–21
  blackening of, 119, 121
  characteristics of, 51–53, 65, 86
  and cultural deficiency/deprivation, 48
  and culturally relevant pedagogy, 79–
    82
  definition of, 50
  diversity among, 103–4
  and gender issues, 90, 99, 100, 103–12,
    113, 114–22, 125
  and "good," 103–7, 112, 115, 117
  and Hmong identity, 85
  importance of money to, 71–72
  interpreting, 84–86
  as invisible, 67
  isolation/marginalization of, 69, 79, 84
  and making "good" schools, 126
  and methodology for research study, 22
  names of, 84–85
  peer influence on, 104–5
  perceptions of education of, 62, 72–73,
    74–75, 84, 116–17, 118, 120
  and poverty, 70–72
  and process of Americanization, 65, 73
  and race, 66–70, 77, 81, 84, 85, 86,
    112, 118, 124
  re-creation of identity and culture by,
    85
  relationship between "Traditional" and,
    53–55, 65, 86, 124
  resistance to culture of whiteness by,
    69, 72–75
  as second generation, 49, 52, 65–86
  self-image of, 74
  silencing of, 78, 79
  stereotypes of, 66, 67
  as stigmatized, 124
  and teachers who care, 79–82
  women as, 103–12
Appiah, A., 7
Apple, M., 34, 35

Asian Americans
  and "Americanized" youth, 103, 115,
    116
  and becoming racialized Americans, 3–7
  characterizations of, 4
  and cultural deficiency/differences, 44,
    48
  exclusion of, 8
  and gender issues, 90, 91, 92, 103, 112,
    115, 116, 121
  as "good," 5
  honorary whiteness of, 5–6
  marginalization of, 4
  mixed-race, 112
  as model minorities, 5, 6, 123
  as perpetual foreigners, 4–5, 6, 7, 22,
    44, 123
  and popular culture, 70
  quietness of, 91
  and race, 3–7, 112
  and reproducing racial hierarchy, 33
  stereotyping of, 5, 6, 92, 112, 116, 121,
    123
  as un-American, 6–7
  See also specific nationality or culture
Asian Club, 27, 30, 53–54, 73, 115
Assimilation
  accommodation without, 120, 121, 124
  acculturation without, 10
  and becoming racialized Americans, 4,
    7–11, 12
  cultural, 8, 9
  and cultural difference/discontinuity,
    42–43
  failure of, 8
  and gender issues, 120, 121
  and intergenerational conflict, 84
  reconsideration of theories of, 7–11
  segmented, 9, 10, 124–25
  socioeconomic, 8
  straight-line theories of, 8, 10, 11
  as threat to Hmong culture, 50–51
Au, K., 41

B4 (singing group), 85
"Bad"
  African Americans/blackness as, 4, 5, 46
  "Americanization" as, 6, 7, 9, 107–12,
    116, 118–21, 125

"Americanized" youth as, 50, 69, 73,
    82–84, 103, 107–12, 118–21
  characteristics of, 50
  and cultural deficiency/deprivation, 46
  and gender issues, 103, 107–12, 118–21
Balibar, E., 7, 48
Banks, J. A., 34
Bankston, C., 2, 9, 50, 52, 54, 73, 125
Barney, G. L., 98
Barth, F., 53
Beck, R., 13, 15
Bell, D., 3
Bennett, C. I., 34
Blacks. See African Americans
Bourdieu, P., 29, 38, 39, 70
Buendia, E., 38, 61

Cammarato, J., 66
Celebrities, Asian/Asian American, 70
Centrie, C., 20, 71, 74, 94
Cha, B., 125
Chan, S., 4, 12
Cheung, K., 91
Child abuse, 51
Chinese/Chinese Americans, 4, 5, 6, 48,
    62
Class, socioeconomic, 18, 22, 60
  and African Americans, 68–69
  and "Americanized" youth, 68–69, 81
  and becoming racialized Americans, 3–
    4, 6–7, 9
  and cultural deficiency/deprivation, 46,
    48
  and curriculum, 81
  and gender issues, 87, 88, 90
  and "good," 46
  hierarchy of, 68–69
  and meaning of whiteness, 23–24
  and privileging "good" parents, 35–36,
    39
  privileging of White middle, 79
  and race, 6–7, 22, 123, 124
Clifford, J., 20
Clothes
  and Americanization, 52, 53
  of "Americanized" youth, 65, 69, 75,
    79, 103, 110, 112, 113, 115, 116,
    118, 119, 120, 121, 124
  and "bad," 50

and cultural deficiency/deprivation, 46,
    47
  and gender issues, 90, 91–92, 100, 102,
    103, 110, 112, 113, 115, 116, 118,
    119, 120, 121
  and "good," 50
  and intergenerational conflict, 82–83
  of "Traditional" youth, 52, 53, 61, 102
Cohn, M., 14, 96
Collins, P. H., 89
Comer, J. P., 35
Community, 2, 9, 21, 128
  See also Hmong Americans
Connell, R. W., 89
Consumer culture, 54, 89, 120, 121, 128
Crenshaw, K. et al., 3
Crosland, K., 38, 61
Cultural deficiency/deprivation, 44–48,
    57–58, 92, 93–94, 123
Cultural difference/discontinuity, 7, 41–
    44, 48, 92, 93
Cummins, J., 11
Curriculum, 3, 32, 34–35, 57, 58, 81,
    126–27, 128

Dance, L. J., 119
Danico, M., 66
Dating, 104, 108, 110, 111
Delinquency, 51, 52. See also Truancy
Delpit, L., 57, 82, 128
Diversity Days, 30–32
Doerfler, J., 35, 36, 38
Donnelly, N., 12, 50, 95, 96, 98, 120
Doumbia, F., 38, 61
Dropouts, 14, 96, 97, 110
Dunnigan, T., 14, 64
Dyer, R., 3, 39

East Asian Americans, 6, 29, 48, 74, 90,
    123
Eckert, P., 24, 28, 29, 72, 90, 103
Education
  and "Americanized" youth, 103, 106,
    107, 115, 116–17, 120
  and becoming racialized Americans, 9,
    15
  as means for resisting racism, 127
  as means of social mobility, 60, 72, 117,
    118

Education (*continued*)
  moral, 38
  perceptions of, 60–61, 72–73, 74–75
  and "Traditional" youth, 100–101, 102–
    3
  of women, 63, 84, 94, 102–3, 106, 107
Eisenhart, M., 89, 105
Epstein, J. L., 35
Erickson, F., 21, 41, 78, 128
ESL programs, 18, 123, 128
  and academic achievement, 75–76
  and "Americanized" youth, 76, 77
  criticisms of, 75–76
  and cultural difference/discontinuity,
    43, 44
  financing of, 59
  and gender issues, 94, 100, 101, 102
  isolation/marginalization of students in,
    58, 61
  and role of faculty and staff in
    reproduction of culture, 27
  as safe space, 55–59
  stigmatization of, 28, 43, 61, 77
  and teacher-student relationship, 59
  and "Traditional" youth, 52, 53, 55–59,
    61, 62, 63, 86, 100, 101, 102, 126
Espiritu, Y., 8, 74, 88, 93, 112
Ethnicity, 8, 9, 10, 18, 31–32, 42–43, 74,
  84–85
Extracurricular activities, 2, 48
  of "Americanized" youth, 53–54, 66,
    69, 115, 117–18
  and defining "talented" and "good"
    students, 28, 29, 30
  and gender issues, 89, 90, 115, 117–18
  of "Traditional" students, 53–54

Faderman, L., 11, 12, 50–51, 65, 95, 96,
  97, 98
Fadiman, A., 81
Families, 9, 12, 18, 79, 128–29
  and Americanization, 50–51, 52
  of "Americanized" youth, 82–84, 85,
    103–4, 106–10, 113–18, 120
  and "bad" and "good," 50
  barriers between school and, 36
  changing roles in, 82, 83, 97–98
  and cultural deficiency/deprivation, 45–
    46, 47
  and economic forces, 97

  and gender issues, 97–100, 101–4, 106–
    11, 113–14, 115–18, 120
  influence of school authorities on, 83
  involvement of, 35–37, 39, 40–41, 46
  and perceptions about education, 60, 84
  popular images of American, 99–100,
    101, 106
  privileging "good," 35–41
  reputations of, 108
  resistance to, 110, 111
  and role of faculty and staff in
    reproduction of culture, 27–28
  and "Traditional" youth, 52, 59, 60, 62–
    63, 101–3
  views about assimilation, 50
  See also Intergenerational relationships
Fass, S., 13, 14, 15, 97
Feagin, J., 3, 5, 6, 72, 88
Femininities, 88, 89–90, 91, 97–112, 122
Ferguson, A., 66, 92, 119
Fine Arts Week, 30–31, 35
Fine, M., 20, 35, 59, 71, 78
Fish, A., 14, 64
Fiske, J., 39
Foley, D., 29
Fordham, S., 20, 75
Frankenberg, R., 3, 24, 39, 40, 44

Gallagher, C. A., 40
Gangs, 15, 70, 74
  and "Americanized" youth, 51, 52, 66,
    67, 69, 73, 83, 84, 116, 119, 121
  and cultural deficiency/deprivation, 46,
    47, 48
  and gender issues, 91–92, 116, 119, 121
  and intergenerational conflict, 83
Gans, H., 8, 9
Gender issues
  and African Americans, 92, 99, 115,
    119, 121
  and "Americanized" youth, 90, 99, 100,
    103–12, 113, 114–22, 125
  and "bad," 103, 107–12, 118–21
  and changing gender norms, 97–98
  and creation and re-creation of gender
    roles, 96–97
  dominant messages about, 88–89
  and economic forces, 97
  and "good," 97, 100, 102, 103–7, 112,
    113, 115, 116, 117–18

messages from Hmong American
community about, 95–98
and methodology for research study,
19, 21, 22
peer influence on, 104–5
and popular culture, 99–100, 101, 106,
107, 108–9, 110, 111, 120
and race, 22, 87, 88, 90, 92, 95, 118,
121, 123–24
and relationships between genders,
112
and sexual issues, 97–98, 102, 107, 108,
109
and socioeconomic class, 87, 88
and "Traditional" youth, 99, 100–103,
113–14, 121–22
See also Femininities; Masculinities
Gibson, M., 9, 10, 11, 50, 51, 60, 84, 102,
107, 108, 109, 124
Gillespie, M. A., 89
Gilroy, P., 7
Gitlin, A., 38, 61
Goldstein, B., 14, 44, 63, 96
"Good"
"Americanization" as, 6–7, 51, 103–7,
114–18
and "Americanized" youth, 79–82, 103–
7, 112, 113, 115, 116, 117
Asian Americans as, 5
and becoming racialized Americans, 3,
4, 5–6
and cultural deficiency/deprivation, 46
definitions/characteristics of, 3, 29, 50,
123, 129
and gender issues, 97, 100, 102, 103–7,
112, 113, 115, 116, 117–18
parents as, 35–41
and race, 123–29
schools as, 2–3, 126–29
and socioeconomic class, 46
students at University Heights High
School as, 28–30
and teacher-student relationship, 79–82
teachers as, 128
"Traditional" youth as, 50, 64, 100, 102
whiteness as, 4, 23, 24, 46
Goodwin, A. L., 34, 128
Gordon, M. M., 8
Gotanda, N., 3
Grant, C. A., 34, 127

Greenhouse, S., 90
Guinier, L., 88

Hall, K., 67
Hall, S., 53
Heath, S. B., 29, 41
Hein, J., 97
Hendricks, G., 14, 64
Hess, R., 44
Hip-hop culture
and "Americanized" youth, 65, 69–70,
75, 79, 83, 84, 85, 86, 112, 118,
124
as "bad," 69–70
and gender issues, 91–92, 112, 118
Hispanic Americans, 42–43, 45–46. *See
also* Latinos
Hmong American Free Press, 75
Hmong American organizations, 97, 129
Hmong Americans
blackening of, 6, 7, 15, 22, 47–48, 65,
66, 123
characteristics of, 13–14
cultural flexibility/fluidity of, 10, 14,
63, 64, 85, 125
as cultural threatening to Americans, 7,
14
diversity among, 21, 54–55, 115–16
"foreignness" of, 123, 124
hiding of Hmong culture by, 124
as inferior, 49
and influx of new refugees, 16
and interference from outsiders, 102
interpretations of cultural experiences
of, 41–49
invisibility of, 13
isolation/marginalization of, 2, 3, 21,
24, 30, 32, 36, 41, 48, 116
as model minority, 64, 86
overview about, 11–16
perceptions of, 14–15, 90–95
stereotyping of, 13, 47–48, 60, 66, 67, 99
withdrawal from Hmong culture of, 116
See also "Americanized" youth;
"Traditional" youth; *specific topic*
Hmong Cultural Club, 28, 30, 31, 53–54,
67, 73–74, 80, 82
Hmong National Development, Inc., 13
Hmong Resettlement Task Force, 16
Ho, J., 70

Hobbel, N., 92
Hoffman, C. M., 34
Holland, D., 89, 105
Hurtado, A., 44
Hutchinson, R., 12

Identity
  and Americanization, 51, 52
  of author, 18–20
  and cultural difference/discontinuity,
    42–43
  ethnic, 8, 74
  factors in considering, 18
  formation of, 1–3, 10–11, 22, 50–86,
    124
  and Hmong as model minority, 64
  oppositional, 9, 11, 70, 83, 84, 85, 86,
    121, 124, 125
  re-creation of, 85
  of teachers and staff, 129
  See also "Americanized" youth;
    "Traditional" youth
Ignatiev, N., 4
Ima, K., 13, 14, 44, 96, 120
Immigrants
  European, 7–8, 42–43
  quotas on, 8
  and "second-generation decline," 9
  stigmatization of, 2
  as threat to American society and
    culture, 7, 14
Intergenerational relationships, 1, 10, 21,
    37, 125
  and "Americanized" youth, 52, 82–84,
    85, 108, 110, 120
  and gender issues, 98, 99, 108, 110, 120
  and "Traditional" youth, 52
  See also Families
Internet, 109, 110–11
Islam, N., 4

Jaret, C., 4

Kailin, J., 34
Kao, G., 9
Kelley, R., 46, 69, 70, 119
Kenny, L., 32
Kibria, N., 62
Kimmel, M., 88, 90
King, J., 34

Koltyk, J., 15, 19, 63, 64, 72, 111
Koreans/Korean Americans, 48, 55, 99
Koza, J. E., 46
Kumashiro, K., 90, 91, 92
Kurien, P., 64

Ladson-Billings, G., 81, 128
Language, 10, 11, 18, 83, 128
  and "Americanized" youth, 69, 75–76,
    114
  and cultural differences/deficiencies,
    42, 46
  and gender issues, 91, 114
  and "Traditional" youth, 55, 57, 58, 61,
    63, 76
Laos, 11–12, 15, 16, 95–96, 98, 101, 108,
    113, 114
Lareau, A., 24, 35, 36, 38
Latinos, 18, 43, 47, 83. See also Hispanic
    Americans
Lee, G., 11, 14, 48, 55, 64, 68, 74, 85,
    127
Lee, Robert, 6, 88, 91, 92
Lee, S. J., 2, 5, 11, 12–13, 15, 18–20, 45,
    47, 63, 97, 101, 103, 127
Lefkowitz, B., 29
Lei, J., 2, 44, 68, 88, 91, 92, 109
Lewis, A., 34, 127
Lewis, O., 44
Lipman, P., 46, 95
Loewen, J., 5
Lopez, N., 94
Loutzenheiser, L., 20
Lowe, L., 4, 5, 44, 85, 125
Lynch, A., 45, 112, 118

Marcus, G. E., 17, 20
Marriage, 14, 18, 19, 21
  and "Americanized" youth, 103, 104–5,
    107–12, 114, 117
  and cultural differences/deficiencies,
    45, 47
  forced, 109
  and gender issues, 93, 95–103, 107–12,
    114, 117
  and ideal husbands, 105, 108–9
  "in Hmong tradition," 111
  interracial, 112
  political nature of, 111
  and "Traditional" youth, 100–101, 103

Masculinities, 88–90, 92, 97–98, 113–21, 122, 125
Mason, J., 41
Matute-Bianchi, M., 9
McIntosh, P., 39
McLaren, P., 44, 127
Meritocracy, 71, 123
Metz, M., 38
Mexican Americans, 11, 29–30, 52, 80
Model minorities, 5, 6, 64, 86, 123
Mohatt, G., 41
Money, importance of, 71–72
Morality, 38, 88
Motherhood, 14, 15, 90–95, 96, 97, 99, 100
Motivation, 45–46, 60
Moua, M. A., 103
Multicultural theater group, 30, 117
Multiculturalism, 11, 27, 32, 33, 34, 126–27
Mydans, S., 16

Nakayama, T., 5
Names, 19, 84–85
Ngo, B., 15, 63, 108, 110
Nieto, S., 31, 34, 35

Oakes, J., 58
O'Connor, C., 127
Ogbu, J. U., 9, 55, 60, 75, 101
Okihiro, G., 5, 6
Olneck, M., 8, 23
Olsen, L., 2, 11, 27, 28, 54, 58, 59, 61, 67, 76, 99, 108, 127
Omi, M., 3, 42
Ong, A., 3, 6, 7, 15, 48, 72, 88, 123
Oppositional identity, 9, 11, 70, 83, 84, 85, 86, 121, 124, 125
Orenstein, P., 90
Osajima, K., 5, 112

Page, R. N., 58
Paradise (singing group), 75
Parent Teacher Student Organization (PTSO), 35
Parents. See Families
Park, K., 2, 4, 55
Park, R., 8
Pascoe, Peggy, 88
Patriarchal system, 94, 95, 96, 101, 122, 124

Patrilineal system, 12, 96
Patriot Act, 7
Pedagogy, 58, 79–82
Peers, 2, 104–5
Perry, P., 32, 70, 90, 127
Pfeifer, M., 12–13, 15, 100
Philips, S., 41
Popular culture, 14–15, 89, 127–28
    American family images in, 99–100, 101, 106
    and "Americanized" youth, 107, 108–9, 110, 111, 120
    and gender issues, 99–100, 101, 106, 107, 108–9, 110, 111, 120
    See also Television
Portes, A., 8, 9, 10, 51, 52, 62, 82, 83–84, 102, 107, 124–25
Postsecondary plans, 15, 81–82, 89, 100–101, 114, 117, 119, 128
Poverty, 18, 22, 95, 123
    and "Americanized" youth, 66, 70–72
    and becoming racialized Americans, 4, 6, 9, 15–16
    and cultural deficiency/deprivation, 44, 46
    and "Traditional" youth, 70
Preissle, J., 34
Proweller, A., 53
Pyke, K., 99, 111, 127

Race
    and becoming racialized Americans, 1–2, 3–7, 8–9, 10, 16
    and cultural racism, 7, 14, 48
    definitions of, 24–25
    and denial of racism, 40–41
    dominant messages about, 1
    and education as means for resisting racism, 127
    and gender issues, 22, 87, 88, 90, 92, 95, 118, 121, 123–24
    and "good," 123–29
    hidden injuries of, 112
    and hidden racism, 40
    hierarchy of, 2, 32–35, 123, 126
    and identity formation, 2, 18, 124
    importance/impac of, 1, 14
    and institutionalized racism, 24
    and interracial relationships, 2
    lack of awareness about, 129

Race (*continued*)
  and methodology for research study,
    21, 22
  and process of racialization, 3, 10, 123
  and racism as hostile acts, 24, 40
  and relationship between "Traditional"
    and "Americanized" youth, 55
  and schools as sources of information, 2
  as social construct, 4
  and socioeconomic class, 6–7, 22, 123,
    124
  and stereotypes, 123
  and White-Black dichotomy, 3–4, 5, 6,
    7
  See also specific topic
Rains, F., 39
Refugees, 6, 7, 16
Resistance
  of "Americanized" youth, 84, 110, 111,
    118, 120, 121
  to culture of whiteness, 72–75
  Diversity Days as act of, 31
  and gender issues, 110, 111, 118, 119,
    121
  and methodology for research study, 19
  to parents, 110, 111
  to racism, 127
  to schools, 2, 11, 110, 111, 118, 119,
    120
Roediger, D., 4
Role models, 28, 34
Rong, X. L., 34
Ruiz, R., 42
Rumbaut, R., 8, 9, 10, 13, 14, 44, 51, 52,
    62, 82, 83–84, 96, 102, 107, 120, 124,
    125

Schools
  "Americanizing" of immigrants as
    function of, 8
  and becoming racialized Americans, 2,
    3, 10–11
  culture of, 3, 23–49
  and gender issues, 118, 121, 122, 124
  "good," 2–3, 123–29
  resistance to, 2, 11, 110, 111, 118, 119,
    120
  as sources of information, 2
  See also Dropouts; Truancy; University
    Heights High School

Scott, G., 15
Second-generation, 9, 11, 18. *See also*
  "Americanized" youth
Sexism, 93, 94
Sexual issues, 97–98, 102, 107, 108, 109
Sherman, S., 14
Shipman, V., 44
Sleeter, C., 34, 42, 127
Smith-Hefner, N. J., 108, 109
Smith, L., 7, 20
Snyder, T. D., 34
Song, M., 62
Sontag, D., 7
Southeast Asian Americans, 51, 74
  blackening of, 6, 7
  and cultural deficiency/deprivation, 45–
    46, 48
  and defining "talented" and "good"
    students, 29–30
  and gender issues, 90, 92, 97, 119
  as perpetual foreigners, 7
  and privileging "good" parents, 37, 38
  quietness of, 92
  resettlement of, 12
  See also Hmong Americans
Sports tournaments, 65, 74
Stacey, J., 20
Staff. *See* Administrators/staff
Stanton-Salazar, R., 81
Stewart, A., 44
Suarez-Orozco, C., 60, 68, 83
Suarez-Orozco, M., 55, 60, 62, 68, 83, 107
Sung, B., 62

Takagi, D. Y., 3
Takaki, R., 4, 5
"Talented," 25, 27, 28–30
Teacher-student relationship, 2, 29, 59
  and "Americanized" youth, 73, 77, 78–
    82, 115, 117, 119–20
  and gender issues, 90, 100, 115, 117,
    118, 119–20
  and "good" teachers, 79–82
  and "Traditional" youth, 100
Teachers, 3, 20, 24, 128, 129
  and "Americanized" youth, 69–70, 76–
    77, 78
  as caring, 77, 79–82, 117, 128
  and gender issues, 91, 92, 93, 94, 122, 124
  "good," 79–82, 128

and privileging "good" parents, 37–38
and racism, 32, 33–34, 77, 129
role in reproduction of culture of, 26–
  28
trust of, 68, 78–79, 128
women as, 94, 120
See also Teacher-student relationship
Television, 105–6, 111, 127–28
Thao, P., 11, 14, 16, 73
Thorne, B., 53, 90, 105
Tienda, M., 9
Tillman, L., 20
Torres, G., 88
"Traditional" youth
  and African Americans, 61–62
  arrival in U.S. of, 52
  aspirations of, 100–101
  characteristics of, 51–53, 55, 64, 86
  definition of, 50
  dual frame of reference of, 55
  and ESL program, 52, 53, 55–59, 61,
    62, 63, 86, 100, 101, 102, 126
  family obligations of, 62–63
  and gender issues, 99, 100–103, 113–
    14, 121–22
  as "good," 50, 64, 100, 102
  and Hmong identity, 85
  and importance of education, 100–101
  isolation/marginalization of, 61–62
  and making "good" schools, 126
  and methodology for research study, 22
  as 1.5 generation, 18, 52, 55–64
  and perceptions of education, 60–61
  politics of being, 63–64
  relationship between "Americanized"
    and, 53–55, 65, 86, 124
  women as, 100–103
Truancy, 50, 52, 60
  of "Americanized" youth, 67, 73, 79–
    80, 83, 119, 120
  and cultural deficiency/deprivation, 46,
    47
  and gender issues, 119, 120
  and intergenerational conflict, 83
  and privileging "good" parents, 36, 37–
    38
Tse, L., 58, 76, 83
Tsing, A. L., 2, 7
Tuan, M., 4, 5, 6, 7, 8, 44
Twine, F., 20

United Refugee Services, 37
University Heights High School (UHS)
  culture of, 21–22, 23–49
  gender issues at, 89–90
  interpretations of Hmong American
    experiences at, 41–49
  methodology for research about, 16–21
  mission of, 25, 27
  multicultural education at, 27
  overview about, 16–18
  parents at, 35–41
  reputation of, 2–3, 23, 24, 25–26, 27,
    60, 126
  role of faculty and staff in reproduction
    of culture at, 26–28
  social hierarchy at, 68–69
  "talented" and "good" students at, 28–
    30
  weaknesses of, 126–28
Urban youth of color, 9, 65, 103. *See also*
  African Americans; Clothes; Gangs
U.S. Census Brueau, 12

Valdes, G., 28, 36, 38, 43, 58, 76, 128,
  129
Valenzuela, A., 2, 9, 11, 50, 52, 54, 59,
  73, 76, 80, 83, 128
Vang, C., 16
Vang, H., 100
Vang, K., 98, 108
Vaught, S., 103, 127
Verma, R., 54
Vietnam War, 12, 13, 16
Vietnamese, 9, 99
Vo, L., 66

Waldinger, R., 8
Walker-Moffat, W., 14, 45
Waters, M., 4, 8, 42, 50, 52, 55, 60, 62,
  64, 66
Weiler, K., 39
Weis, L., 20, 71, 74, 94
Welfare, 3, 14, 15, 16, 66
Whites/whiteness
  and American-ness, 4, 8, 35, 49, 123
  and "Americanized" youth, 66–68, 71,
    72–75, 112, 115, 116, 117
  as authentic Americans, 55, 124
  and becoming racialized Americans, 3,
    4, 6, 7, 8

Whites/whiteness (*continued*)
  celebrating culture of, 30–32
  characteristics associated with, 23
  and defining "talented" and "good," 28–30
  distrust of, 68
  dominance of, 23, 39, 40–41
  and gender issues, 88, 89, 90, 112, 115, 116, 117, 121
  and "good," 35–41, 46
  insidious influence of culture of, 49
  and interpretations of Hmong American students' experiences, 41–49
  invisibility of, 4, 39, 40, 43–44
  and making "good" schools, 127, 129
  marriage to, 112
  meaning of, 23–24
  as norm, 3, 39, 48, 123
  oppositional identity of, 70
  parents of, 35–41
  privileging of, 3, 22, 24, 35–41, 42, 77–78, 79, 127, 129
  as real Americans, 127
  and relationship between "Traditional" and "Americanized" youth, 55
  and reproducing racial hierarchy, 32–35
  and role of faculty and staff in reproduction of culture, 26–28
  stereotypes of, 49
  superiority of, 79, 112
  and "Traditional" youth, 61
  and White-Black dichotomy, 3–4, 5, 6, 7
  See also Race
Willis, P., 71, 72
Wimps, perception of Hmong youth as, 90–95
Winant, H., 3, 4, 5, 7, 24, 42, 48

Women
  as "Americanized" youth, 65, 103–12
  aspirations of, 100–101, 102, 104, 112
  "bad," 107–12
  and becoming racialized Americans, 14
  blackening of, 95
  and characteristics of Hmong culture, 14
  and cultural deficiency/deprivation, 44–45, 47
  devaluation of, 96
  education for, 63, 84, 94, 102–3, 106, 107
  family obligations of, 63
  feminities among, 92–95, 98–112
  "good," 102, 103–7, 112
  and ideal husbands, 105, 108–9
  and intergenerational relationships, 84
  quietness of, 92–93
  and race, 124
  "safe spaces" for, 94
  and selective acculturation, 63
  silencing of, 95
  as subordinate, 93, 120
  as "Traditional" youth, 100–103, 121–22, 124
  as victims, 93, 94, 122
  views about schools of, 124
  weight of, 112
  See also Gender; Marriage; Motherhood
Wu, Frank, 5, 7, 24

Xiong, G., 11, 12, 50–51, 65, 95, 96, 97, 98

Yang, K., 100

Zhou, M., 2, 9, 50, 52, 54, 73, 124–25

About the Author

Stacey J. Lee is Professor of Educational Policy Studies at the University of Wisconsin-Madison. Her research focuses on Asian American immigrant experiences. She is the author of *Unraveling the "Model Minority" Stereotype: Listening to Asian American Youth*, published by Teachers College Press.